To Mr. Lyttleton
with Many Thanks
for two years Tutorage!

Angus McLlyn.
        Eton 1994.

HUGH JOHNSON

on

gardening

Hugh Johnson On Gardening

First published in 1993
by Mitchell Beazley
an imprint of Reed Consumer Books Limited
Michelin House, 81 Fulham Road
London SW3 6RB
and Auckland, Melbourne, Singapore and Toronto

Editor: Emily Wright
Designer: Jeremy Roots
Production: Sarah Rees

Executive Editor: Anna Mumford
Art Director: Jacqui Small

Wood Engravings by Jonathan Gibbs

ISBN 1 85732 303 3

A CIP catalogue record for this book is available from the British Library

Printed by Bath Press, Bath, Avon

These extracts were first published in *The Garden*, the journal of the Royal
Horticultural Society. Please note that facts and figures may have changed since the
time of writing.

HUGH JOHNSON

on

gardening

The best of Tradescant's Diary

THE ROYAL HORTICULTURAL SOCIETY

CONTENTS

INTRODUCTION

It is 18 years now since I started the monthly preface to the RHS journal which (for reasons revealed within) has come to be known familiarly as 'Trad'.

The inauguration of a diary column in what had always been an extremely staid publication came as a bit of a shock to its readers. At the time the whole journal was going through a radical change. It had maintained more or less the same format and severe appearance for a century. Strange to recall that it had to justify itself becoming (relatively) glossy. The RHS is not a revolutionary organization: many old RHS members preferred the chrysalis to the butterfly.

As time passed, though, Trad's monthly assignment became about as stressful as pulling on an old patched coat for a garden sortie.

To have a persona slightly outside himself (or perhaps just a little to one side) is a luxury for a writer. At least this one. Ideas for 'Trad' crop up all the time: in conversation, musing alone, being struck by some happy combination of plants – or indeed outraged at some horticultural abuse. When copy date approaches (too long before publication, alas, for any item to be punchily up-to-date) there is always a sheaf of possibilities. The ones that feel most comfortably like the old coat are the ones that tend to go in.

When I started 'Trad' I asked a wide range of gardening friends to try to remember to send me snippets of information, rumours, anything that might be worth following up. One or two did, once or twice. But it has been the readers who have continually supplied me with grist to the mill; readers from wherever the RHS has members – and the moon seems to be the only place it hasn't.

Re-reading the 18 years' worth of diary, picking what I hope are plums with my editors, has brought the changes of a generation vividly into focus. How incredibly far-off seem some of the assumptions and preoccupations of 1975.

In the 1970s garden history, now a booming academic industry, was of interest only to a deeply recondite clique. Conservation did not arrive on the horticultural agenda until 1978 – via, I am happy to say, a special issue of *The Garden*. We had nowhere near the choice of plants we have today, or of gardens to see them in. Who remembers now that there was (briefly) a garden in Covent Garden, or the battles we fought over Wisley Airport, over the Hanbury Gardens at

La Mortola, or indeed the eccentric weather of past years which sent up cries of a new ice age – rapidly to be followed by shouts of global warming.

It has all had an entertaining side, and Trad has been very lucky to have gardened, and wandered in gardens worldwide, through such times of change, pricking up his senses at each season, with the beauties, the follies, the threats and the successes that it brings.

My thanks then go first to the Chairman of the RHS Publications Committee, the late Lord Blakenham, who originally invited this potential cuckoo into the RHS nest; to the three editors who have tolerated Trad: Elspeth Napier, Susanne Mitchell and now Ian Hodgson; but most of all to the readers who continue to egg Trad on. May your ground elder evaporate and roses perfume your life.

1975

—July—

OUR PATRON

Who was Tradescant? There were two Tradescants of horticultural note, father and son, both called John, both Royal Gardeners to Charles I and both among the most illustrious names of English gardening in the seventeenth century. Between them they introduced a number of important plants from Russia (some say it was Tradescant senior who introduced the larch), from Mediterranean countries and Virginia, where Tradescant junior went three times.

In their own collection at Lambeth they grew some of the first American plants in Europe, among them virginia creeper, spiderwort (*Tradescantia virginiana*), the swamp cypress and the tulip tree. Tradescant junior gave his collection of 'natural and artificial curiosities' to his friend Elias Ashmole, who in turn presented it to Oxford University, where it became the basis of the Ashmolean Collection.

Why take their name in vain? Because it is not likely to be confused with any other. There is no Tradescant in the London telephone book. Nor, for that matter, is there an Ashmole. More's the pity.

THE COVENT GARDEN GARDEN

For sheer horticultural enterprise it is hard to beat the new garden which has transformed part of the wasteland behind Covent Garden in the last year. This is the first new public garden in the centre of London for over a century.

The site, on Endell Street, had been a car park for 27 years. The Covent Garden Open Spaces Action Committee had the temerity to see capabilities in its 1¾ acres of 14-inch concrete. What they achieved (at first entirely by cajolement and persuasion, only latterly with the help of grants) is astonishing.

An artesian well, said to be part of the old Fleet river, was the clue to the possibilities. Breaking up a third of an acre of concrete for the lake was the most expensive item. Thereafter McAlpine's gave clay excavated from the new Fleet Line to line the pond and brought 120 tons of topsoil from another site for planting. The broken concrete was formed into hillocks on the solid concrete floor to provide drainage and the topsoil was put on top.

The garden was designed by Keith Cheng, an actor and exhibition designer. It is clearly Japanese in inspiration: a make-believe landscape of sinuous lines, a complete break with traditional London square planting. The Japanese embassy has clearly taken it as a compliment: they have joined in enthusiastically with designs for the paving.

Not all the planting is exactly planned. There are 60 birch trees which were used in an industrial exhibition and were too precious to throw away. And sophisticated notions of restful foliage patterns are elbowed aside by well-wishers with lupins or wall-flowers to offer 'for the flower-beds' – so flower-beds there have to be.

Alas the garden is unlikely to live long, for this central city site is too valuable. But even if it disappears in a year or two it will have given great pleasure, both to those who wander and sit in it and to the volunteers who do the work – even to the trout and carp whose job it is to keep the water clean.

Above all it will have shown that there are better things to do with two acres in the centre of a city than park cars on them.

—October—

LOOK YOUR LAST

Outside my window stands a heart-wrenching 80-foot reminder of the greatest natural disaster to have struck this country since the war: the death of the elms. These magnificent healthy trees in their full autumn glory are a shade of gold no other tree attains, a colour which elms can hold, in a good season, for six weeks on end.

It has been a summer of bitter attrition in lowland England. The Forestry Commission has gloomily confirmed that this is the worst year yet. They hold out one straw of hope: that the ferocious newly introduced fungus which is doing the worst damage may interbreed with the old strain, which has been mildly at work here since the '30s, to produce a less virulent variety.

In 1971 the government put up £250,000 to help local authorities combat the disease. In January 1973 they officially declared the fight hopeless, confining themselves to efforts to stop the disease gaining a hold in counties it had not yet reached – preventing unbarked elm logs, for example, from entering unaffected areas.

But that is all that has been done. No money is available for clearing away the millions of dead trees, trying to stop the rest dying, or for replacing the loss with new trees.

If elm disease were a giant oil slick in the Channel, funds would be found to fight it, and no questions asked. But because it works steadily, never hitting any one day's headlines, the government has been able to ignore it. It is high time it took action.

A Plaque for J.I.

John Innes already has as good a memorial as any gardener could wish for: is not his name invoked in every potting shed in the land?

Notwithstanding, the Greater London Council is to put a blue plaque on his old home, the Manor House in Watery Lane, Merton, quite rightly to remind passers-by that J.I. was not only the arch compost-maker (or indeed, as far as the GLC cared, the compost-maker at all). J.I. is known in Merton as the enlightened developer who built a very handsome suburb, planting it with splendid trees and hedges which still flourish – particularly his favourite: holly.

In his will, J.I. directed his executors to found either a museum or a school for horticulture and it was not until 1909 that the Charity Commissioners published a scheme which established the John Innes Horticultural Institution at Merton. This was the world's first institute for scientific investigation of gardening problems. The first Director was William Bateson, a pioneer of genetics in this country. The work on compounding the classic compost formulae was done in the 1930s.

Until 1946, when air pollution drove it into the country, the Institute was based at the Manor House. The plaque, therefore, doubly commemorates the home of a wise and generous Victorian and the birthplace of scientific horticultural research.

—November—

Aftermath of a Drought

With almost every garden in the country gasping with drought by late summer, the question everyone wanted answered was how much permanent damage such a baking does. If a young tree or shrub shrivels, if its leaves turn brown and fall by, say, late August, is that the end? Can it recover and make a good plant?

The answer is not a very cheerful one. There are plants which seem to be able to cope, making their resting buds and dropping their leaves as in autumn but as much as a couple of months early. Some even manage fleeting autumn colour in August. But, by and large, a tree overly drought-stressed and forced to shed its leaves in mid-season is seriously weakened by the ordeal, and a newly planted tree or shrub is set back so much that its growth rate will be affected for years; indeed it may never make a really fine specimen. Conifers in dry areas often have a thin and weedy look because they have shed their older needles on inner twigs and branches. They can never get them back: the result is a poor-looking tree for the rest of its life.

This particular year has been the devil because the dry summer followed such a wet winter. The deeper roots of trees in badly drained ground may well have perished, placing more of a burden on the surface roots – the very ones short of water this summer.

The moral of all this, at least as far as new planting is concerned, is to plant in generous holes of good soil, early on in the season, not at the last minute before bud-break, and above all to plant small. The heart-breaking sight of new trees standing dead (so common along roads, particularly this year) could be avoided if planters put them in at three to four feet instead of eight to nine. Obviously there are places where the threat of vandalism makes this impossible. But in gardens and the countryside small trees start best and grow fastest into fine specimens.

Moreover small trees are cheaper: a useful point for local authorities.

— *December* —

WAYWARD TENDRILS AT WYE

England lies at the northern limit of the zone in which the grapevine can usefully be cultivated out of doors. Which side of the limit it lies is a hotly debated point. Enthusiasts claim there is nothing to prevent England re-establishing the vineyards she had in the Middle Ages, when every monastery and many manors made their own wine.

The reason for their decline, they argue, had nothing to do with the climate: it was England's acquisition of Bordeaux, by royal marriage in

1152, which gave us a bigger and better supply of wine on English ground (albeit in France). English wine-making became unprofitable.

Nobody really knows, of course, what the climate was like nor how it has changed since. But we do know that modern summers, with such rare exceptions as 1975, leave something to be desired. Wine can rarely be made from English grapes without added sugar. Breeders have done wonders recently in producing early-ripening varieties, but to make good wine you need more than just ripe grapes: you need the right natural sugar-acid balance.

Add to the natural difficulties the fact that English wine growers have to pay the same preposterous duty (48 pence a bottle) as wine importers, and it is clear that only determined characters need apply.

Notwithstanding these problems, however, the Ministry of Agriculture's figures for last year show that there were 414 acres of grapes grown for wine-making in England and Wales, which is more than there has been since the Middle Ages. The English Vineyards Association is a thriving body with about 375 members, and research into the best methods, varieties, rootstocks, pruning systems and other techniques (essential in a country which has no traditions, no background of trial and error) is in hand at Wye College in Kent and at Efford Horticultural Station in Hants. Wisley also has a demonstration vineyard, now three years old, which has borne good fruit this year.

LÈSE-MAJESTÉ

There has been a serious outbreak of banality in Granada. Visitors to the Alhambra this year have been appalled by the new planting scheme in the Court of the Lions. The original Moorish garden, I believe, consisted of beds two feet below the level of the paths, so that carpet bedding looked, literally, like carpets, with the flowers at ground level. The exquisite stone tracery and the solemn beasts are now beset with a gallimaufry of plants of stupefying irrelevance: *Salvia splendens*, *Senecio laxifolius*, even spotted aucubas.

The planting was instigated in 1973 by the Historic Gardens Committee of the International Council of Monuments and Sites, which held its conference in Granada that year. It is a comfort to learn that the committee of seven included not one single British member, but not so comforting to imagine what they may be up to now.

1976

—January—

WINTER FUEL

The world is much the poorer for the lost technologies of earlier times, when it was common knowledge, for example, exactly which wood was good for what.

I came across this translation of a Latin poem on the properties of firewood. It appeared as a letter to *The Times* on 1 March, 1929.

Beechwood fires are bright and clear, if the logs are kept a year.
Chestnut's only good, they say, if for long its laid away.
Make a fire of *Elder* tree, death within your house shall be.
But *Ash* new or Ash old is fit for a queen with a crown of gold.
Birch and *Fir* logs burn too fast; blaze up bright and do not last.
It is by the Irish said, *Hawthorn* bakes the sweetest bread.
Elm wood burns like churchyard mould; e'en the very flames
    are cold.
But *Ash* green or Ash brown is fit for a queen with a golden crown.
Poplar gives a bitter smoke, fills your eyes and makes you choke.
Apple wood will scent your room with an incense-like perfume.
Oaken logs, if dry and old, keep away the winter's cold.
But *Ash* wet or Ash dry a king shall warm his slippers by.

—February—

AN EXCURSION

It is always an enlightening experience to take an excursion into the opposite season of the year. In November I visited May, not in H.G. Well's time machine, but with the International Dendrology Society touring Patagonia and southern-to-middle Chile in the full flush of the southern spring.

One of the most spectacular visits was to a pure forest of *Araucaria araucana* (which I shall never again demean with the name monkey-puzzle) at 5,000 feet on the slopes of the volcano Llaima. We saw the trees through an intermittent blizzard. The snow made their simple prehistoric geometry all the more compelling: they seemed like vegetable dinosaurs. Unlike dinosaurs, however, they are far from extinct, or even threatened. In their own country they are doing fine, with the younger generations following on their parents and grandparents as vigorously as ever. The biggest of the old trees is almost 150 feet high: one of the world's most marvellously ugly vegetables. But the young playing at their parents' feet often have a whimsical charm.

One group of trees we were looking at gave our grave gathering of dendrologists much amusement. John Codrington, with his deep knowledge of arboreal nature, told us that the young fellow on our right was a sort that nice young araucarias avoid, and that the girls knew it and were retreating in giggles to their governess.

—April—

EYE-OPENER

A reader reacted quite petulantly to an article on willows by writing to ask who would waste space on mere willows; one willow, he averred, being much like another. I hesitated to retort that the same could be said of rhododendrons unless you opened your eyes to all the marvellous differences. But the sentiment is clear enough: a plant without flowers that shows up at a distance is not worth a place in the garden.

At this moment my little collection of willows is the one thing worth braving the weather to see. In the summer their fantastically varied leaves will give me another distinct pleasure. The Japanese, who know a good plant unerringly, do wonderful things with them. But enough of willows...and more about the Japanese.

My brother brought me from Tokyo an American book called *Japanese Gardens For Today*, by David H. Engel, which has utterly enthralled me. After a dozen crisp chapters of introduction it consists of excellent black- and-white photographs, mainly details, of Japanese gardens ancient and modern, big and (the majority) small. The details are a feast. The paving, screens, still small pools, carefully placed rocks, single pines, stepping stones, clumps of bamboo, eaves and porches and lanterns, pots of chrysanthemums, massifs of moss – every cranny shows acute visual awareness.

To a Japanese gardener the way we pack bright colours together, almost apologize for any parts of our gardens which are not jammed with flowers, must seem childish. His senses are already awake; they don't need violent stimulus to start registering. And his senses are backed up with such vivid imagination that swirls of sand round a group of little rocks can carry him beyond the Hebrides.

CONNECTICUT

Dr Niering, the Director of the Connecticut Arboretum, sent us a booklet that preaches the gospel of long grass. Under the rather woolly title of Energy Conservation on the Home Grounds, it is a vehement tract against lawns, on which Americans spend $3 billion a year and use more fertilizer than is used on all the agricultural land in India.

First it gives case histories of gardeners who gave up mowing and found true happiness in the resulting grassland. The text and pictures together are remarkably convincing. I am not about to scrap my mower, but I do now wonder why I waste time and fuel smoothing out certain areas of the garden which would look just as good, and certainly more interesting, rough.

I rather like the little anti-mower story the author tells: one Friday evening a householder in a Washington suburb stopped at several of his neighbours to borrow their motor-mowers. By the time he collected the third its owner asked him what he planned to do with all the mowers. 'Get a good morning's sleep' was his answer.

GARDENS ON VIEW

Rachel Crawshay, the indefatigable organizing secretary of the National Gardens Scheme, has every reason to be proud of this year's yellow book of gardens to visit, which has been on the bookstalls since last month. It can't have been easy to keep the price down to the same very reasonable 30 pence as last year. And more remarkable still is the fact that the same number of gardens will be open, despite all the difficulties which beset ambitious gardeners these days.

If anything, there is a trend towards groups of small gardens ganging together to open – which, to the gardener of a small patch, can be more stimulating than broad acres he knows he can't emulate.

Small wonder that garden-visiting is becoming one of the country's most popular spectator sports. There is quite simply no other way of learning so much about possibilities (and pitfalls). Every good garden has ideas pinched from other gardens. There is nothing to be ashamed of in copying a successful piece of planting – except of course it never will be an exact copy. Often it will gain something in the translation.

I confess to carrying both camera and notebook – in fact behaving like a fully fledged spy – in other people's gardens. The greatest joy is in gardens which have a plant stall on the way out (and there are commendably many that do) to carry off a piece of precisely the plant you so admired, already growing happily for you.

I shall rush (or maybe join the queue) to see the Mill House at Sutton Courtenay, reflected in its lake and framed in roses, summing up everything that makes early summer in England nature's last word. I will also seek a glimpse of The Aviary in Berkshire, the Gertrude Jekyll-designed water garden at Vann in Surrey, and the splendid herbaceous borders at Brynderwen in Gwent.

Next year the National Gardens Scheme will have been going for 50 years. I can hardly think of any other voluntary organization which will have given so much pleasure.

— May —

CHELSEA

The fruit-salad effect of the Chelsea Flower Show this year is unmistakable. There are so many good things looking their best at the end of May that only the strongest-minded nurseryman can resist a grand gallimaufry. And what a joy they are, these gardeners' shop windows. I can already smell that marvellous mingling of azaleas and peat and roses and excitement which fills the marquee. Last year I arrived at opening time, 8.30, on the Wednesday morning, as the sun began to suck up the dew. A sight and scent not to be forgotten.

There can never really be a proper preview of Chelsea. Too many things depend on spur-of-the-moment decisions. Particularly flowers which have had to be either advanced or retarded to be at full voltage at exactly the right moment.

From the information I received in March, though, we can look forward to as gorgeous a show as ever, with a number of exciting new plants and a host of ideas for saving time, labour and money – besides, of course, making your garden more beautiful and satisfying than ever.

—June—

PERPETUAL MOTION

What we call alternative technology (and the Victorians called common sense) can have few better examples than the old hydram water pump. Few things of man's invention, in fact, have come nearer to the alchemist's dream of perpetual motion. In brief, what the hydram does is to pump water by harnessing water power. Using no fuel, no electricity, no outside energy, it moves a small steady stream of water to where it is needed, activated simply by the flow from a modest source.

I have just been restoring an old hydram which was installed, so its makers tell me, in 1920. I had only to ring them up and give them the serial number and within two minutes they were telling me about it from their records. The flow of water from the spring (20 gallons in a minute in 1920; still the same today), the length of the delivery pipe (450 yards; still the same), the height of the outlet (60 feet above the pump), and the volume of water delivered: 1,300 gallons a day, or getting on for a gallon a minute.

All my aged pump needed was a rusty pipe replacing and a new valve; now we have what appears to be a natural little rill running merrily over rocks and splashing into a pool in our formerly arid garden. The water goes back into the ground, thence into the spring, whence back into my stream.

The miracle is performed by collecting the spring water in a tank with a four-foot head above the pump (which is partly sunk in the ground). The flow from the tank down the 'drive-pipe' presses on and intermittently opens a heavy brass valve, which then shuts again naturally by its own weight. Each time the valve shuts a small proportion of the water in the drive-pipe is forced by the recoil through a non return valve into the delivery pipe. Nineteen-twentieths of the water flows away to waste, but the remaining precious twentieth is the water in my perpetual, free stream.

Nothing goes round, nothing needs oiling, nothing (touch wood) goes wrong. Even more important, meanness apart, my conscience wouldn't let me run an ornamental stream which consumed precious energy. Whereas my perpetual motion stream is a constant source of amusement and wonder. Wonder, most of all, why one hears so little of what must be the dream of all ecologists.

THE SOUTHERN BEECH

When (and I say when rather than if) *Nothofagus*, the beech of the southern hemisphere, becomes a familiar and important tree in Britain, it will largely be due to the efforts of one exceptional and visionary tree-lover, the Earl of Bradford.

I have been visiting his experimental plantations near Tavistock and in Shropshire, where several *Nothofagus* species (but principally two from South America: *N. obliqua* and *N. procera*) are matched against the fastest-growing trees in current use: Douglas fir, thuya, redwood, western hemlock. In most cases the *Nothofagus* is growing at twice (literally twice) the speed of its nearest rivals. In a plot of seven-year-old trees the thuya might be 20 feet tall; the *Nothofagus* will be 40 feet.

Seed of these trees, which grow in limited zones in the southern Andes and round Valdivia in Chile, is not easy to acquire. In a dense forest, with an undergrowth of 12-foot bamboo and berberis, collecting the tiny short-lived seed of the tall beeches is almost impossible. One way is to make a clearing and fell a big tree heavy with seed, but the organization to mobilize resources in remote roadless country doesn't exist. Or didn't until Lord Bradford made it his business. As a result of his indefatigable correspondence there now seems to be a good chance of the first substantial shipment in the near future.

At Weston in Shropshire, Lord Bradford keeps what as far as I know is a unique 'forest garden'; some 30 acres divided into ¼-acre plots in which he plants combinations – sometimes seemingly rather improbable ones – of trees to see how they get on together. His unwearying observation of the results at close quarters is constantly producing new information. Different rooting habits, different periods of leafing, different rates of spreading to form a canopy and exclude light from the ground are the sort of factors which influence growth. There are successes and failures, but the greatest success by far are the *Nothofagus*, which outstrip any other tree or combination of trees.

To the ecologist, to the nature conservationist, to the hiker or lover of landscape, the potential of the southern beech is wonderful news. It means that if all goes well the next generation of forest planting in this country (on most soils; not all) will be deciduous, and indeed indistinguishable in overall effect from our native hardwoods. A forest of southern beeches will be as beautiful and natural-looking in Sussex as it does in Patagonia.

For gardeners their rate of growth and their light and graceful canopies will make them indispensable. Even for street planting they will be ideal: they move well at big sizes and their small leaves are easily cleared and composted. *Nothofagus* can grow 20 feet in four years from seed.

— *July* —

LIME LOVERS

The Alpine Garden Society's Bulletin this spring contained an article which must have come as a shock to many keen and well-intentioned growers of alpines. It pointed out that all that lovely creviced and mossy 'water-worn Westmoreland' in such tempting heaps in garden centres has to come from somewhere, and that the somewhere is usually a limestone pavement, one of the irreplaceable landscape features of northern Britain.

The pavements, exposed outcrops of limestone, were laid bare over ten thousand years ago by the glaciers of the last Ice Age. Since then water has eroded them in deep grooves which provide a specialized habitat for many rare species of lime-loving plants. Natural rock gardens, in other words, are being destroyed to create artificial ones.

— *October* —

CLAREMONT

Following the restoration of the seventeenth-century garden at Westbury on Severn and the model, shown at Chelsea this year, of plans to reinstate the original garden design at Ham House, the National Trust unveiled this summer the start of its most ambitious garden restoration yet: the grand layout at Claremont in Surrey in which all four of the greatest garden designers of the eighteenth century, Vanbrugh, Bridgeman, Kent and Brown, were involved.

Surrey in the early years of the eighteenth century was freely compared by its aristocratic inhabitants with the groves of ancient Greece. Gardening on the grandest scale was the fashionable pursuit.

When Sir John Vanbrugh sold his Esher property to a fellow member of the Kit–Cat Club (who, becoming Earl of Clare, christened it Claremont), it is easy to imagine the pleasure such a group of talented men of taste took in planning the grounds.

Bridgeman is credited in particular with the great four-in-hand avenues, the round pond (which he repeated later in Kensington Gardens) and the inspired 'amphitheatre' of sculpted earth. Vanbrugh designed the belvedere – thought to be the earliest mock-medieval building in England – and the winding woodland walks with their leafy vistas back to the focal point.

Later modifications to the design were made by Kent for the Duke of Newcastle (as Clare became) and Brown for Clive of India, who owned the property briefly in the 1770s, before it became a royal retreat, which it remained for most of the nineteenth century and up to the death of the Duchess of Albany in 1922. In 1930 the estate was split up and the gardens fell into decay.

The National Trust now owns 50 acres of the pleasure grounds which are managed for them by Elmbridge Borough Council. Their initiative in restoring the overgrown gardens was prompted by a munificent grant from the Slater Foundation. Surrey is fortunate indeed. As if the classic groves of Wisley were not feast enough.

— December —

BAD NEWS

Garden conservation seems to have been a recurring theme this year, and we end 1976 with two reports on this subject: a happy one and, unfortunately, a sad one.

The sad news concerns the Enfield garden of the great E.A. Bowles, known, by reputation at least, to all gardeners. His garden at Myddelton House is sadly neglected, and those who knew it in its Bowles days can hardly bear to enter it now. But even if they wanted to go, the present owners, the Lea Valley Regional Authority, do not feel it is necessary to open the garden except on very few days in the year. Local residents, and the local horticultural society (founded by Mr Bowles) feel particularly hurt at their exclusion, for in Mr Bowles's day they were made welcome.

Worse still, the garden is becoming a wilderness, with the rock garden being strangled by brambles, a padlock on the door of the conservatory and a new path across the lawn in pink crazy paving. Poor Mr Bowles.

The Lea Valley Regional Authority do not, apparently, realize that they are in control of what to gardeners is an almost sacred plot. Their achievements in designing the Lea Valley Country Park may well be a feather in the Authority's cap, but Bowles's garden is a skeleton in their cupboard. Members who live nearby may feel inclined to see it for themselves and let their local authority know what they think.

GOOD NEWS

After such a depressing story it is a relief to turn to Sissinghurst Castle, so admirably managed by the two head gardeners there, Pam Schwerdt and Sybil Kreutzberger. It is always in perfect condition, and they have learned to cope with wear and tear to the garden that is inevitable with the thousands of visitors now coming to the garden, originally planned for the Nicolsons and their family. One part of the garden at Sissinghurst which has suffered over the years is the paving in Harold Nicolson's spring garden. This was a compromise; when it was laid 40 years ago, concrete paving was used. With the trampling of many feet above and the roots heaving them up from below, the paving was becoming less and less satisfactory, so a bold decision was made by the National Trust to replace the paving with York stone.

The common limes originally planted in the paved area have also been unsatisfactory, for two reasons. Although traditionally recommended for pleaching, this species attracts aphids, which cover the plants and the ground beneath with sticky honeydew, and it also grows suckers all the way up the trunk. Another lime, *Tilia euchlora*, has neither of these disadvantages and responds to pleaching equally well. So, with admirable foresight, the Trust bought some young trees about five years ago, which have been trained on wires in the nursery. This winter they will be planted out when the paving is renewed. The operation should be done with a minimum of disturbance to the bulbs in the borders at the sides, and to the visiting public, as all should be finished by the start of the season next April.

1977

—*January*—

SURVIVORS' CLUB

Silver and grey plants are among the most widely praised by people who have already (by the end of October) responded to my paragraph about the drought. Let me thank scores of readers for their very helpful observations, a quarry of information from which we hope to hew a useful article.

Meanwhile I have just noted some of the plants that keep recurring as better than survivors; plants that took the drought as a cue for their best performance. Not all, by any means, are accepted drought-lovers.

Both camellias and magnolias were reported from all sides as showing no signs of thirst. Oddly enough, liquidambars were noted by several people as flourishing (they are usually said to be trees for moist ground). One I know certainly produced better autumn colour than ever. Walnuts were predictably prolific. The 'paperbark' maple, *Acer griseum*, has never looked happier.

At random, among herbaceous plants, sedums and euphorbias (a wide range, but especially *E. robbiae*) were two of the summer's heroes. Agapanthus, alstroemerias, salvias of many kinds (but not *S. patens*, which barely flowered or grew until the September rain), bergenias, paeonies, sea lavender, stachys, pyrethrum, *Astrantia major*, *Zauschneria cana*, valerian, crocosmia, *Clematis heracleifolia*, daylilies, rosemary, rue and many herbs, *Malva moschata*, *Macleaya cordata* and hellebores all flourished unrained-on and unwatered.

Roses were mentioned a great deal by the papers during the drought as doing much better than one would expect. Perhaps for this reason relatively few Members have reported outstanding performances by their roses.

Shrubs praised by many people include ceratostigma, iberis, helianthemum, choisya (healthy throughout, then flowering superbly when the rain came), caryopteris, red (not black) currants, *Eucryphia* × *nymansensis*, many hebes (but not *H. armstrongii*), berberis and mahonia, brooms, euonymus, ceanothus and cotoneasters.

Among annuals, petunias and tobacco plants managed a good show with their roots in unmoistened dust. Among vegetables, calabrese and Alicante tomatoes have been mentioned several times, and many people seem to have had a normal crop of potatoes. (One Member magisterially remarked; 'A healthy soil should always be able to contend with differing weather conditions'.)

Rhododendrons I have not mentioned. It was not their summer. But from what people say of the flower-buds on the survivors it should certainly be their spring.

—February—

ONE SOLUTION – SIMPLIFY

A telling sign of the chronic shortage of gardeners today – and a masterly solution. Russell Page, who gardens in the grand manner if anyone does, was saying recently that he is limiting himself to three elements in the work he is doing now. All his plans are based on water, grass and trees. Skilled and willing gardeners for more intricate planting, he says, can't be found.

Yet, when you come to think of it, the idea is not so much limiting as liberating.

—March—

NOW, AT LAST!

There are many schools of nursery catalogue-writing. The time-worn superlative is perhaps the most familiar. There is also the sedate, the scientific – even the priggish scientific, full of little slaps on the wrist to non-botanists – and (at the other end of the scale) the simpleton.

But in one school of composition, which I can only call the Circus Programme, Thompson & Morgan, the old and indispensable seed-merchants of Ipswich, stand alone.

For a sample of the style my favourite item is: 'Perhaps the last truly great new plant discovery in the entire flower kingdom. To grow and experience the sheer prehistoric beauty of its startling floral shape and gunmetal blue colouring is quite profound.' (sic). We are speaking of the seaholly *Eryngium* 'Delaroux' (*E. proteiflorum*). Of course.

—April—

ARIZONA

I spent a bright wintry day recently with the ebullient Beth Chatto in her rapidly expanding nursery-cum-garden near Colchester. I recommend it at any season as one of the most stimulating outings a gardener can take. Amid retrenchment on all hands, this remarkable lady is in the process of enlarging her garden, fields at a time.

Last summer's efforts added two more to the chain of ponds she has engineered in her shallow valley by interrupting a modest brooklet. The latest two are the most imposing of the lot, and with the adjacent oak wood will add a new dimension to what is already a marvellously varied garden.

Mrs Chatto's first appearance at Chelsea last year with her stand of 'Unusual Plants' put every garden sleuth in the country on her trail. Not least *The Sunday Times*, who visited her in mid-drought, saw the arid slope she calls 'Arizona' looking like a million dollars, and promptly commissioned her to design a drought-proof garden for the newspaper. It appeared in June, and her resulting fan-mail has not entirely died away yet. The direct result is that she is writing a book on dry gardening, which as an Essex gardener with a gravel hill she is well qualified to do.

If an indirect result is that next summer breaks all records for rainfall I shan't be entirely surprised.

Our own drought post mortem (presaged in January) has not, as you might think, got bogged down. We have decided to hold on until we can be sure that life really has passed away. Autopsies on several apparent fatalities have proved premature.

—June—

SILVER JUBILEE

Thank goodness Jubilee Year has given the press another reason for talking about planting trees. We desperately need them, yet journalists will never acknowledge the fact in isolation: it always has to be tied to some story – some excuse.

I can't keep up with all the Jubilee plantings we are hearing about. But one worth looking forward to is an additional development of an acre at the Savill Garden at Windsor – basically, I'm told, with trees and shrubs selected for their autumn colour. Sir Hugh Casson is also designing a new footbridge across the bottom pond to be installed later this year.

—*July*—

'THE JUNE GAP'

There have been one or two references recently to 'the June gap' which have rather puzzled me. The implication is that there is a dull patch in gardens in the month of June. Roy Hay said as much in *The Times* one Saturday last summer: that there was very little to pick for flower arrangements. I must admit I don't find it so: June is almost our floweriest month. But a correspondent who lived in Italy many years ago puts a new construction on it. She speaks of *la giuntura* – the joining gap – at the end of May and the start of June, when subsistence farmers in poor areas like the Abruzzi had finished the previous year's harvest, and nothing of the present year's was yet ready.

Presumably the same gap used to apply to the poor in England. Surely this is where the term comes from then, rather than any lack of flowers?

COVENT GARDENING

Eighteen months ago I wrote with enthusiasm about the Covent Garden Open Spaces Committee, the enterprising group who were making a Japanese garden on a derelict site in Shelton Street. The land was originally lent to them by the GLC until such time as it was needed to build flats. That time has now come and the pagodas give way to the bulldozers.

Nothing daunted, its creators are in the process of making two more gardens in the area. The Earlham Street chess garden is right on the pavement. Surrounded by newly planted deciduous and evergreen shrubs and trees, and overlooked by an enormous mural by Stephen Pusey depicting on a nearby building the local people's struggle with the land, the chess lover may sit down at one of the small concrete chess tables and have a quiet game.

The second garden is still at the development stage and is in Bow Street, behind the Royal Opera House, to whom the land belongs. This will be an Italian garden. F.W. Collins, the Earlham Street iron-mongers, are the leaders of this excellent piece of horticultural initiative. Besides that, they are first-class ironmongers of the old-school, refreshingly free from packaging and full of useful hardware. Incidentally, they sell splendid bamboo poles of all shapes and sizes.

—August—

FOREIGN ROOTS

It is a breathless Trad you read this month: still panting with excite-ment after two weeks in Japan, absorbing a notion of gardening so totally different in its essentials from what we practise that it leaves radical questions germinating like cress.

Japanese gardeners garden above all for the permanent picture. They will go to any lengths to perfect a view and then any lengths to keep it precisely so, unaltered year after year. Also season after season – the bones of the garden are evergreens, and, of course, rocks in bewildering profusion and variety.

On the stage, so to speak, of this static garden, seasonal changes become dramatic happenings. Starting with the great festival of cherry blossom, when the whole country is an operetta orchard with people in their best clothes picnicking and dancing under the pink-frothy trees. Then the massed ranks of azaleas, clipped into rigid forms which seem incongruous as they burst into flower. Then irises by the water, with the tame carp in their brilliant motley cruising between them to make a startling picture. And so on to the year's climax when the maples smoulder and blaze in gardens and woods.

Gardening for the plants' sake, for the love of flowers, seems like a secondary strain – indeed a different discipline altogether. This is the common man's form of gardening. It consists of careful clusters of pots: a bonsai tree in one, an azalea in another, a spotted aucuba in a third; in a fourth a weird strain of morning glory with etiolated brown petals or multiple mauve ones.

A pot satisfies the Japanese eye as much as (or perhaps more than) a border. Just as each dish in a meal is served separately, often exquisitely, in a tiny bowl, so I suspect a Japanese would find our riotous borders like our meat and two veg with plenty of thick gravy: a gross and inexplicable waste of good things by mixing them together.

With such talented and industrious gardeners around I was truly surprised to learn that only last year did Japan get an amateur horticultural society of its own for the first time. I was lucky enough to meet its founder-president, Dr Tsukamoto, who has recently retired from Kyoto University.

I asked Dr Tsukamoto what were the favourite plants of his 2,300 members and was rather taken aback to be told cacti: perhaps the most exotic plant in a country of high rainfall. Chrysanths are high on the list; also camellias and primulas. Roses are rare – though the few I saw were exceptionally well grown, and, of course, perfectly trained.

Dr Tsukamoto has a fascinating hobby. He collects references to garden plants in the fine arts. His filing system is a journey through the world's painting and carving, pottery, porcelain...tracing the development of the pink or the tulip through its appearance in Buddhist shrines, Flemish tapestries, Persian bas-reliefs; anywhere anyone has faithfully recorded its form.

He took me to a great Kyoto monastery to see the sixteenth-century ceiling panels of flowers on a soft gold ground; a specimen to each panel: lily, iris, clematis, *Rosa chinensis*, cherry, paeony, bamboo...score upon score of perfect plants. The paper screens dimmed the light and gave the colours on gold a mysterious luminous quality. I have never seen anything lovelier.

—*September*—

DERELICT

I continue to get letters from readers who are upset by the state of E.A. Bowles's garden at Enfield, which I wrote about in December. Despite local and national representations, and even an offer of funds, the Lea Valley Regional Authority continues to keep this historic garden so woefully understaffed that it mocks the gardeners' most heroic efforts.

The name of Bowles means so much to so many gardeners that it seems particularly sad that his life's work should be allowed to decay.

I had another melancholy experience recently visiting the final remnants of the great garden of Fulham Palace, where Bishop Compton assembled one of the first collections of North American plants in Europe. Here again there were signs of dedicated work, especially in the herb beds (there is a charming relic of a box-edged garden), but the overall state of the place is appalling; pieces of fine statuary lying among undergrowth; walls crumbling; greenhouses glassless and tottering; a big beech, stone dead in the middle of the lawn. What is wrong with an age which can't even afford to keep the basics – walls and glass – in repair? It took a visit to the immaculate Cambridge Botanic Gardens (of which more shortly) to recover my spirits.

AS SHE IS SPOKE

Tradescant turns out to be one of those words that people think twice about before pronouncing. The natural way seems to me to be to stress the first syllable, Trad. One scholarly school of thought puts the accent on the second.

Perhaps they are right. Just as those who pronounce Miss Jekyll's name with a long 'e' undoubtedly have right on their side.

I must confess, though, that the correct forms make me uneasy when they single out the speaker from everyone else as one who knows better. Who really knows, anyway? Who knows how Shakespeare, a contemporary (nearly) of Tradescant's, pronounced his name? He spelt it any number of ways. I'm afraid to me Jekyll is Je'kyll, and Tradescant is Tra'descant. For that matter, clematis is clematis. The OED says so and that's enough for me.

— October —

SHADES OF EVENING

There comes a moment on a summer's afternoon, some time after tea, when the shades begin to quicken and the dryads to leave their nooks. The sun, which bleached all colour from flower and leaf while it stood overhead, lets the pigments flow back as it inclines towards the west.

Alas, this is the hour when the bell rings and the paying guests must take their leave.

It struck me forcibly this mid-summer, as I tried to pack three Sussex gardens into a single day – an economic necessity – that opening times could be more thoughtfully arranged than they are.

Few gardens open their gates before 11am, which means that not only does a visitor miss the pearly light and the morning dew, but he has only the chance of one garden before lunch – and that he must see it with the sun at its zenith, a hopeless time for photography.

After lunch he will have to sprint to see two...and then be shown the door just at the witching hour.

Obviously staff difficulties have a great deal to do with it. But could not a little imagination find a way of letting the public occasionally see our best gardens at their best?

— December —

FOR ENTERPRISE

My private (and hitherto secret) gardener-of-the-year award goes this year to an entire family: the de Belders of Kalmthout, Belgium. Their arboretum at Kalmthout has been famous for many years. But this autumn I went to see where Robert and Georges and Robert's wife, Jelena, are forming Europe's most ambitious private arboretum on 300 acres of cool green pasture at Hemelrijk near the Dutch border.

The first planting took place in 1964 against a background of the soaring oak and beech avenues of a demolished château. When we saw them in September, in company with a hundred members of the International Dendrology Society (which the de Belders helped to found), celebrating the Society's Silver Jubilee, it was almost impossible to believe that the tall healthy trees grouped in their families round the calm grey lakes are no more than 13 years old.

The concept of Hemelrijk approaches a private Kew of woody plants. The many seed beds contain the fruit of countless expeditions to collect seed in the wild – including thousands of *Rhododendron yakushimanum* from the de Belders' expedition to Japan's wild southerly island in 1970.

It is an exhilarating experience to pant after one of the family on a headlong tour of such a thriving young collection. Quite different from a reverent perambulation of one of England's mature arboreta.

AQUARIUS

Our drought of '76 seems very small beer beside the horrific situation which has confronted California this year.

Two years almost entirely without rain has made the conventional green garden, maintained by sprinklers, a total impossibility. In some areas – worst of all in Marin County, the leafy suburban area just north of the Golden Gate – whole gardens have died and had to be cleared away because of the fire risk...And what do you do with dead shrubs when you can't burn them for fear of setting the whole neighbourhood on fire?

The admirable quarterly *Pacific Horticulture* published an issue on the drought in the autumn. It contains some wise words on gardening within the natural plant range (ecology, if you must) of the area. California's first gardens, it points out, were patios like those of central and southern Spain. A little water made a great show in a shady enclosure and could be put accurately on plants that needed it. None was just thrown about. Basic planting was all in drought-resisting natives or imports from the Mediterranean.

Then settlers from the east brought their taste for English-style gardening. Ironically it was a sequence of drought and flood in the 1860s which killed millions of cattle and made the great ranchers sell their land cheap to the immigrants.

In place of restrained and suitable planting the new arrivals took advantage of California's (fairly) reliable warmth to mix every conceivable plant in a mad jumble regardless of origin and thirst. Taste has improved, but the paradox of green sward in the desert remains – or did until this year. Now it has turned brown California has an opportunity to find a garden style which leaves out, or carefully segregates, water-demanding plants.

Knowing Californians, they are likely to rise to the challenge brilliantly. Knowing California, on the other hand, they are just as likely to be washed out next year by a mighty flood.

We just don't know how lucky we are.

1978

— *January* —

OUGHT COTTAGERS TO GROW FLOWERS?

The Pleasure Garden is the title of Anne Scott-James's lucid little history of our way of gardening which came out in the autumn. Osbert Lancaster's mesmerically apt set pieces are the framework for a series of essays in which, as in good gardening, art conceals much hard graft (OED meaning 2: hard work, derived from digging, cf. grave).

Her chapter on the cottage garden, in which she rightly says, 'it has been a bastion of tradition, a sanctuary for plants trembling on the verge of extinction, and an inspiration for gardens larger and finer than itself', reminded me of a cutting our editor Elspeth Napier dug out of her hoard, an article in *Gardening for the Million* by George Glenny, 1862 (by which time the title page tells us he had reached 120,000). The title is 'Ought Cottagers to Grow Flowers?'. Glenny has doubts. 'The idea of tempting poor men to grow Pansies, and Pinks, and Carnations, by awarding them prizes, seems to us downright wicked...Half a dozen pair of pinks...would require more time and attention than a rod of cabbages, potatoes, turnips or carrots.' What were cottage gardens *really* like a hundred years ago? Oh, for a time machine.

— *February* —

DOWN UNDER

Although we all long ago gave up expecting summer to be summery, winter wintry and spring and autumn perfect passages of transition, unseasonal events still come as a jar.

I came home recently from a fortnight in Australia to an early November heatwave in which that lovely pale yellow June daylily, *Hemerocallis flava*, was flowering under the powerful pink of the mid-winter viburnum, *V. bodnantense*. There seemed no reason why everything in the garden shouldn't flower at once, which would give me no pleasure at all. Flowers out of season have the wrong vibrations.

I found this in Australia. It was mid-spring; the air in the miles of marvellous gardens round Melbourne and Adelaide smelling like

Chelsea. I gazed in wonder, interest, awe at the spectacle; yet it failed to click. I was looking at a picture of spring, not the real thing. My system was set for autumn. I realized how plants must feel when we wrench them from one hemisphere to the other.

Click or not, Australia was exciting. Australian gardening is in rude health. Melbourne and Adelaide, already richly endowed with botanic gardens of great splendour and public parks galore, are both making completely new collections on a lavish scale 'in the bush' – i.e. out of town.

Adelaide's new garden is up near the top of Mount Lofty, a more modest peak than its name suggests, overlooking the city from the east and enjoying twice as much rainfall as the coastal belt where the city lies. The 200 acres were opened in November, 17 years after the first planting. It will be primarily a woodland garden in the English sense, with rhododendrons, magnolias, maples, cherries, dogwoods and conifers, spring bulbs and waterside planting around a lake.

Meanwhile the old garden in the heart of the city has a most impressive spread of new order beds set in a broad boulevard of brick paving between splendid old trees – an idea which reminded me of Russell Page's ideal garden in *The Education of a Gardener.*

Intrusive buildings, alas, have spoilt the atmosphere of parts of the garden. The hospital, an unmannerly pile with gaudy red and blue plastic panels, grins down into it from tree-top height. Much could be done with screening trees.

Melbourne has things better organized. A city edict forbids tall buildings near the famous Victorian (in both senses) botanical gardens. The gardens remain an extraordinary elysium: a sort of Eden, indeed, where plants of all climes flourish indifferently; the azalea lies down with the date palm. Melbourne records one (slight) frost a year.

The dramatic sweep of the valley was used to brilliant effect by the designer Guilfoyle in the 1870s. A series of long open lawns, divided by great wedges of trees, rocks and shrubs, run downhill to converge on a long lake of bays, promontories and islands – formerly a meander of the Yarra river (which, straightened, now runs alongside).

One of these lake-islands has recently been christened Stayce Island. Dr David Churchill, the present director, has found evidence that Guilfoyle's plans were not as original as everyone thought. That one Stayce, in fact, an unfortunate competitor of Guilfoyle's, had a considerable but unacknowledged hand in the matter. Stayce disappeared.

Melbourne's new garden is to be an impressive 400-acre park of native Australian plants in sandy hills at Cranborne, south-east of the city. Dr Churchill sees it as echoing the flowering 'English' style of the city garden, with open lawns between massifs of planting. Grass, however, is out of the question. What then is to be the smooth flowing surface? One possible answer, being considered, is simply sand.

— *March* —

HAMMERSMITH

When Tradescant clodhopped into the Fulham Palace Garden (September last) saying rude things about the state of the grounds, he didn't know that it was only four years since Hammersmith Borough Council had leased it from the Church Commissioners, and that at that time it had been in a state of disrepair which is still reflected in the tottering walls and glassless glasshouses. Horticulturally, vast strides have been made in the meanwhile, which is not surprising from the department which regularly wins gold medals at Chelsea. All visitors to the Show will remember the woodland glade. The designer was telling me how preparation started in mid-January with the selection of a huge number of possible plants at the Borough's Mortlake and South Park Nurseries. By mid-April three plans were drawn and one chosen, which left exactly a month to get the best plants in the nurseries up to scratch.

Odd, I remember thinking, that urban Hammersmith should show a woodland garden. To my further surprise, when I went down to the Palace Gardens again recently I found that they really do have one, and a very pretty one, but by the river and rather oddly inaccessible from the rest of the grounds.

CROWN OF HEATHER

The curving beds in the grass round the circle-front of Buckingham Palace must be the most conspicuous bits of garden in the whole country. It is worth recording how splendidly their keepers rise to the challenge of planting the beds in such striking and dignified but long-lived displays.

Usually they are red, representing the rubies in a crown formed by the whole design, as seen from the Palace windows. Last summer the centre beds were an impressive mass of white – tobacco plants and petunias – which went bravely on from late May to late September.

This winter they have been a bonny block of an unusual and very effective heather, a hardy selection (by a German nursery) of the South African *Erica gracilis*, a mass of glowing dull red. Under the heather the red tulips, Diplomat, are ready for spring.

– April –

RED DATA

Not everyone realizes that the World Wildlife Fund is concerned with plants as well as animals. Their panda emblem should have a threatened wild flower behind its ear – or rather between its sheltering paws; not even pandas should pick wild flowers.

The Fund has recently sponsored the publication by the Society for the Promotion of Nature Conservation of a Red Data Book on British plants threatened with extinction. So for the first time we know which of our native plants are threatened and why, and where they are found.

Three-hundred-and-twenty-one plants (out of 1,700 in all) are on the list, over 30 of them unique to Britain. They are categorized in the same way as all threatened creatures in the Red Data Books of the International Union for the Conservation of Nature: as endangered, vulnerable and (merely) rare. The wild flowers, 'weeds', of arable land are in most danger: 96 percent of them are threatened to a greater or lesser degree.

The lowering of the water table by drainage and extraction, and also the excessive use of fertilizers are threatening almost as large a proportion of our bog, fen and marsh plants. The Scottish and Welsh mountains have 60 very rare 'alpine' species.

The threats are far greater now than at any time in the past. Since recording began in the seventeenth century, only 19 species are known to have been lost, whereas 46 may well follow them into extinction before the end of this century.

—May—

P.S.

It came to me in a flash as I walked past the Lamb Hotel near the cathedral in Ely the other day. Ely-agnus; Elaeagnus – of course. These botanical mispellings do sometimes obscure derivations that are really perfectly simple.

—July—

An Open Letter to Messrs Spear, Jackson, Wilkinson, Stanley and Bulldog...

Whatever became of the straight spade? I have one; Ted Barrett at Boughton has one; and we would both like new ones. But this most natural and useful tool has disappeared from the market, and all I am told when I ask why, is that spades should be kinked, rather as Father Glum held that 'bathrooms is white; landings is brown'.

The culprit, I believe, is something called ergonomics. The angle of blade to handle saves a bit of pushing and pulling when you are digging solid clods. (What it boils down to, I suppose, is that you don't have to bend so low.)

But digging rows of heavy soft brown earth is only one of the many jobs I do with my spade. Most of the year it is busy digging holes in hard clay criss-crossed with stubborn tree roots. I've tried doing it with one of your ergonomic spades and given it up as a bad job. Your straight spade is as good as an axe, biting deep into virgin clay, severing roots three inches thick. It is also highly manoeuverable for edging, and well-balanced and light as a simple extension to my arm – try reaching out to scuff up the earth and cover your footprints with a kinked spade. I've even trimmed little branches very satisfactorily with its straight sharp edge.

I'm sure you've got the message, gentlemen. I would like you to start making straight spades again. So would Ted. Neither of us is a funny shape. If we find it such a useful tool so would millions of other gardeners.

— August —

LIGHT GREEN FINGERS

From time to time we hear stories which make us wonder if W.C. Field's awful remark – 'Anyone who hates children can't be all bad' – shouldn't have been – 'Anyone who steals plants...'.

Not long ago Archie Skinner, the gardener at Sheffield Park, noticed that two young camellia plants seemed to be mysteriously shorter than before. When he looked closer he found that some dastardly visitor had cut off their tops, flowers and all, dug up the roots, and to cover his get-away, stuck the tops back in the bed.

The desire to possess – the root of all the world's troubles and many of its joys – is particularly well-developed in gardeners. Perhaps we think that because our pursuit is relatively harmless to others we can get away with a little extra petty crime in compensation. But the light-fingered visitor is the despair of everyone who holds open their garden. Even the 'tiny cutting' may be just the very bit the owner intended to use.

My revolutionary suggestion is that if the desire to possess something in someone else's garden becomes overwhelming you should simply ask them if they can spare a bit.

Wilfred Blunt's book on Kew, incidentally, is most illuminating on this murky subject. In Sir Joseph Banks's time, it was alleged, all his new acquisitions were so jealously guarded that it seemed reasonable, almost honourable, to try to bring out trophies. According to the Hon. the Rev. William Herbert, who attacked Banks for his illiberality, 'every private collection' thus 'became exposed to like depredations'.

Could this be the historical reason why even certain upright citizens seem to think plant-stealing is fair game?

I most heartily recommend Blunt's book, *In for a Penny*, as the most elegant, the most succinct, and by far the most amusing guide to the background of Kew. Blunt is an urbane and witty scholar, yet with a sense of justice and reasonableness always wide awake. His historical characters live. His criticisms are constructive. We are lucky to have him as an interpreter of botanists to mortals, and I suspect botanists are lucky to have him too.

— *September* —

GLO-BAGS

The Grobag is here to stay. It is well-established as a horticultural convenience with a score of uses. Last year Fison's dressed a Victorian 'buildings' estate in London's dockland with Grobags of flowers on every iron balcony and turned it into a set for a Neapolitan opera. We are convinced.

But now we are ready for compost-coloured Grobags. *Must* they be printed in gaudy bright red and yellow?

— *October* —

THE DOCKS: A SUGGESTION

There is not much reason these days for anyone to visit the London docks. A dismal deadlock seems to have developed, with dozens of reasons why nothing can be done with a part of London which has immense natural advantages.

It struck me as I passed through the area recently that it provides a fantastic opportunity for a great new garden: a Kew for the East End. I suddenly saw the dock basins rimmed with stooping willows and jewelled with water-lilies. Couldn't a great riverside garden in the east give that whole side of London the uplift it so badly needs, and make desirable a place which nobody seems to want?

If the authorities can't make up their minds about bricks and mortar, perhaps they could agree on the much lesser expense of planting, and provide worthwhile employment in giving innocent pleasure and eventually a whole new lease of life to half of London.

TALKING OF TOOLS

My plan for a straight spade in July seems to have touched a nerve. Correspondents have plied me with fascinating facts about tools.

Before the war it seems there were more than 50 kinds of spades made – more or less one for each county. My straight one apparently was the Leicestershire model.

One correspondent complains that flat-tine potato forks are no longer made, and suggests that country auctions are the best place to look for good old tools, unless one happens to know a retired gardener or a gardener's widow.

Sir Gordon Russell, who was director of the Design Council in the 1950s, writes that his favourite garden weapon was a German First World War entrenching tool. More generally he makes the observation that tools should look right as part of the garden scene. Old zinc or aluminium watering-cans did. Modern plastic ones in lurid colours have to be hidden away.

— *November* —

ELY-AGNUS

I got the reprimand I deserved for my tongue-in-cheek note about the derivation of *Elaeagnus* – not because it was so wrong but because it was so nearly right. Professor W.T. Stearn, who should know if anyone should, tells me that the 'agnus' bit is indeed a reference to sheep. The Greeks used the word for willows because of their woolly catkins. But the 'Ely' part is the really surprising one. Who would believe that the name of the town is derived from the eels in the fens around? Ely, in fact, means eely.

— *December* —

LOOKING BACK

We didn't get much swimming this year, but it's been the best in the garden that I can remember. An astonishing year, with cool days and intermittent rain keeping flowers on for far longer than their usual span. Outstanding performances were far too many to mention – practically everything in fact. At the end of the summer there was such a sustained finale that I made a list of 200 things either in flower or looking like a million dollars.

The grass, of course, at the price of endless mowing, was looking like spring in September, which gave the early-autumn colours an unusually brilliant foil. Embarrassing numbers of apples (though not so many pears) – and even plums, which I had given up hope of seeing on our unkempt old tree, whose real job is holding up a *Clematis flammula* in the path of the evening breezes to perfume the terrace.

Tomatoes were a flop. None ripened at all outside, even on a southwest wall – and I am ill-at-ease about a young eucalyptus that has grown five gangling feet in its second year, and looks green enough to be withered by the first decent frost.

In case someone else's ecstasy is of interest I will do an abbreviated catalogue of the highlights of this late summer in one eastern garden.

Firstly, waving at me through the window as I write, Japanese anemones of unprecedented splendour. I found a first edition of Robinson's *English Flower Garden* on a junk stall not long ago and was delighted to see that he had chosen this prince among flowers to be engraved in gold on the cover. This year they have grown to over six feet and cast a jolly white glow into my study.

Secondly, Beth Chatto's wonderful creamy mini-kniphofia – you can't call it a red hot poker – 'Little Maid'. Very often short plants are notable chiefly for being out of proportion, squat and dumpy. 'Little Maid' is petite in all her parts, and this year, after dividing and what with the rain, has come up with a plethora of pokers. Behind them stands a *Caryopteris*, mistily blue, and growing beside them the grey-pink variegated *Fuchsia magellanica*. The moods of autumn vary from the fiery and strident to the gentle and contemplative.

Thirdly, the long season of the gentian-blue sage, *Salvia patens*. If you grow it from cuttings and plant it out with the dahlias it can be over all too soon. But this cool year has kept up its sprinkling (no more; never a dollop) of sapphire for ten weeks, looking lovely with the yellow of the evening primrose early on, and now serene with the pink tree-mallow – giving another four-star performance.

Overriding all, and perhaps the real reason I am so full of glee about 1978, is the magnificent growth of new trees and shrubs, which for once have had all the water they want. A scarlet oak in its third year has grown three feet in two giant strides. That's what I call a season.

1979

—*January*—

RESOLUTION

Not for the first time I have resolved to do something useful this new year by keeping a garden diary. Not exactly a diary perhaps but a wide-ranging notebook. Experience has shown (to all of us, I expect) that however sure we are that we will remember when something flowered, or which spot needs a touch of excitement at a particular time of year, when the time comes to do something about it we will have forgotten our bright idea. This year I shall write it down.

Performance of fruit and veg, use of fertilizers, vagaries of weather, visits of birds, orders of plants, ideas from other gardens, quotations from books, things seen at shows, snippets from the wireless ('The Natural World' often has priceless asides for gardeners) will all go in my book. Also paragraphs of records about just how marvellous an October morning was, and how it felt to see the yellow nose-cones of *Sternbergia lutea* pushing up through parched earth like a crocus of genius that has discovered something the others don't know.

I'm not at all sure when I shall read it. I will have to underline things requiring action in red ink, or they will be lost in the verbiage.

—*February*—

PLANTSMEN AND THEIR TOOLS

The subject of tools continues to interest my correspondents. From recent letters I have learned the very important intelligence that the sort of straight spade I was lamenting is still available. I should keep my eyes nearer the ground when I go shopping.

Another reader has recommended the old-fashioned spade known as the 'grafter', which has a tapering blade with a half-moon section, to take out a plug of soil: very useful, he says, for digging small holes without disturbing surrounding plants. He also mentions a use for the inevitable fork with a broken tine. He cut off the two outer tines to make a two-tine fork for close work.

I am grateful to another reader for pointing out that a left-hand glove turned inside out is a right-hand glove. To those who asked where to get a greenfly brush such as I described I must apologize: it was a relic of earlier days. I don't know anyone who makes them.

It may help to prevent some of the mountains of elm-wood in the country from being wasted to point out that there is a marvellous machine-driven log-splitter available. Elm can be the very devil to split, but this tool pushes a wedge through it, using a hydraulic ram, as though it were poplar. I hired one for a modest sum and saved weeks of frustrating hammering and many many pounds on fuel bills.

— *April* —

Baptism by Ice

In the public-spirited hope of causing an immediate and lasting thaw, followed by an early spring, I sit in the icy brightness of a room over-looking a snow-bound garden and write about the cold.

Almost everyone has had at least a short spell of true winter weather. It has not been anything to compare with 1963 yet, but it has already put paid to several plants I had been foolishly treating as hardy. I didn't have a garden in 1963, so the experience is new. And so is the shock of discovering that rabbits will eat *anything* after a few days of snow. Trunks of trees unmolested for years have been savagely gnawed. The only evergreen bushes I will now guarantee as rabbit-proof are yew and box. Holly is clearly delicious – especially its bark. Ivy is a treat. Hebes are obviously caviar. Cistus and sage are probably a bit over-seasoned: they are largely ignored.

But as to the cold itself: I wonder what surprises it has brought. I wonder about the eucalyptus of so many kinds that have been settling down nicely in Dorset, for example. I wonder whether my limp and bedraggled *Euphorbia mellifera* will pull through. It has been so long since real cold-hardiness has been put to the test all over the country that it will be interesting to hear of readers' experiences: particularly of doubtfully hardy plants in cold places that came through the ordeal.

—June—

EQUIVOCATION AND OUR OAKS

It is wonderful how civil servants can equivocate when it comes to matters of urgent decision. The threat of the oak wilt reaching this country from North America is very serious. American oak is shipped in large quantities for the Scotch Whisky distillers. The bug that does the damage lives in the sapwood as well as the bark, so merely banning the import of unbarked timber does no good. You would think that the Forestry Commission, who advise the government on these matters, would have learnt a lesson from the fiasco of Dutch elm disease, having failed to recognize that danger until it was too late. But no, they want more time, and consultation with interested parties, before they will simply stop the import of oak from America.

Why does everybody have to be fully satisfied that it is essential? Isn't the mere threat enough? What would it matter if Scotch had a very faintly different flavour a few years from now compared with the tragedy of an epidemic among our oaks?

It is disappointing that the Tree Council, when it discussed the matter in March, could not decide unanimously to press for a ban, but instead moved that urgent investigation should be made to see whether the present safeguards are adequate. We know they are not adequate. They consist of a Forestry Commission man available on call to any customs officer who is doubtful about a load of timber. It is a pound to a penny that all customs officers are doubtful about all loads of timber. They are not trained to know oak from ash. But they are certainly not constantly calling out the Commission's men to examine every load of logs.

The decision should be to ban all American oak immediately and then examine the safeguards. If they can be made good enough the ban can be lifted.

—July—

FAR CATHAY

There is one prospect that quickens the pulse of every red-blooded gardener, and that is the thought that at long last the remoter reaches of China may soon be accessible again. There are already rumours, and more than rumours, of botanical and horticultural expeditions that are preparing to visit the western provinces where E.H. Wilson found so many splendid plants for our gardens at the beginning of the twentieth century.

I once heard Sir George Taylor, who went on one of the last expeditions from the west to the Sino-Tibetan borders, describing the still largely uncatalogued riches of this fantastic country. Species after species of rhododendron, primula, lily and their typical companions clothe the rain-soaked mountainsides and roaring gorges. You can read mouth-watering accounts by Reginald Farrer and Frank Kingdom Ward. Many of the plants have never been introduced to cultivation. Others have been introduced and subsequently lost.

The new mood of China makes it possible that we shall have the thrill our parents and grandparents had of meeting scores of new plants never seen in gardens before. Not that we exploit as we should the introductions which are already here.

—August—

FLOWERS IN ART

We are having an orgy of exhibitions for gardeners this year. I am just in time to recommend that you drop everything to go and see the British Museum's contribution. Under the title *Flowers in Art from East and West* is gathered together a ravishing collection of the best flower portraits ever painted, or in some cases printed.

It starts with lovely pieces of Chaucerian freshness from herbals and breviaries long before he conjured up his 'freshe floures white and rede'. There are consummate pieces of observation by Leonardo and Dürer and all the great European botanical painters from the seventeenth century to today: examples of van Huysam, Ehret, Redouté,

Bauer, Turpin...strongly challenged, amazingly enough, by the work of native draughtsmen in China and India painting to European commissions. The European tradition of the botanical plate is represented here in all its richness.

What struck me most of all about the exhibition, however, is how stiff the Western style seems in comparison with the painting of China and Japan. Basically all Western artists have painted portraits of plants; sometimes prettified, sometimes warts-and-all, but always treating the plant as if it were a sitter.

The oriental tradition of painting on scrolls and screens relies more on design than formal likeness. The sense of life and movement in the way the plants are laid on the silk or paper – even when it is a simple woodblock on an ordinary page – has no western parallel.

The sense of design reaches its height in woodcuts and in the almost calligraphic rhythms of ink-painting: just a few brave brush-strokes to convey the essence of plum or pine or bamboo. Scoring for realistic observation and sense of design, the East wins hands down.

SHOWING THEIR TRUE COLOURS

Personally I see red at the very thought of a non-blue delphinium. Setting prejudice aside, however, I must report that progress in the breeding of red delphinia has been going on nicely at the Agricultural University at Wageningen in Holland. Dr R. Legro has developed the University Hybrids, which include yellow, pinks and a true red. Although at present they are not quite ready to be launched into the rough and tumble of garden life, they last longer as cut flowers in water than the blue ones, which must count in their favour. Unfortunately Dr Legro's money supply (he is sponsored by the Dutch government) is threatened just at the moment when he feels he can overcome their constitutional weakness. He has appealed to the Delphinium Society for help in keeping the strain going. Happily the Society is one of the most active of its kind. It held a symposium earlier this year on the future of delphinium breeding, and will surely take up the challenge.

Incidentally, if you act quickly you can have delphiniums among your Christmas decorations this year. Last year we tried drying them, cutting them in almost full bloom and hanging them upside down in a warm dry room. Miraculously they kept the full potency of their blue, or very nearly. Perhaps the red ones will do even better.

—*September*—

GIARDINO APERTO

In each generation over the past four or five centuries there have been so many new gardens being created that the abandonment of old ones has been a matter merely for nostalgic regret. Not so now. When any considerable garden comes under threat the urge to save it is reinforced by the knowledge that its loss will diminish the global total.

Hence the extraordinary flurry of international activity that resulted, this spring, in saving the Hanbury Gardens at La Mortola, near Ventimiglia and the Franco-Italian border. The munificent Sir Thomas Hanbury not only gave his villa and the surrounding estate, sloping down to the Mediterranean, to the Italian people; he also bought Wisley for the RHS.

At La Mortola he made a very important collection of tender plants that could be grown at few other places in Europe. It has remained an outstanding, if slightly down-at-heel, collection to this day.

I won't go into the chicanery by which it was to become a regional arts centre and public park until the gardeners and botanists of the world get to hear of it. But I have a collection of posters testifying to the determination of the *lavoratori* not to let it disappear, ranging from 'Come back Sir Thomas' to an organized hoe-in, or whatever you would call the refusal of gardeners to stop work.

The happy outcome is that La Mortola is to be under the care of the botanical department of the University of Genoa, which has a first-class reputation.

The next Italian garden to worry about may well be the legendary Ninfa, planted at the turn of the century in the ruins of an abandoned medieval town south of Rome by a Henry-Jamesian family of Italo-Anglo-American stock. Those who know it say it has magical qualities. Few have seen it, and the recent death of the presiding genius may mean that few ever will, unless a rescue operation can be mounted as soon as possible.

—November—

UNDER WESTERN EYES

I paid a visit during the summer to a remarkable gardening institution in California; the offices of *Sunset* magazine. *Sunset* is 'the magazine of western living', a family-run glossy with a unique and admirable record of helping its readers to settle in a part of the world where practically everything and everybody is new. Its service to gardeners is one of the brightest parts of its record. It comes closer, perhaps, to a learned society than a normal glossy magazine in the scope and depth of its researches into plant performance in the vastly varied conditions of the West.

For many years it has had the collaboration of hundreds of observers, both professional nurserymen and keen amateurs, in every corner of each of the western states, from the deserts of southern California, Nevada and Arizona to the cloud-hung forests of Oregon and Washington. Its gardening editors meet groups of these correspondents at regular intervals to compare their notes, draw conclusions (or at least identify interesting questions) and gradually to build up a body of authoritative information about the behaviour of plants, both endemic and exotic, in western gardens.

The fruit of this labour – besides many magazine articles – is the *Sunset Western Garden Book*, whose fourth edition appeared this year. The 350 pages of this book constitute one of the most useful, thorough and easy-to-follow plant encyclopedias I have ever met, so good, in fact, that even in Britain I habitually look things up in it.

Despite the obvious dissimilarities between our growing conditions and those in most of the West, the North-West comes closer to northern Europe than any part of the eastern States, whose climate has a thoroughly continental temperament, that is to say, wildly intemperate in its extremes.

Americans are well accustomed to buying British gardening books and taking their advice with generous pinches of salt. The new *Western Garden Book* is not available here but it would be well worth our while returning the compliment. You will be surprised to find how little seasoning is needed.

1980

—*January*—

A NEW LEAF

Tradescant's resolution for 1979 was to keep records of what happened in the garden: what was planted when, and what the results have been. For the permanent plantings such records are essential, and increasingly interesting and valuable with time. Besides their possible scientific value, there is huge satisfaction, mingled with nostalgia and a pleasant sense of the passing of time, in looking at a towering tree or bulging bush and saying, 'I only planted that seven years ago', even if the next sentence is 'what a pity it has to go'.

With vegetables and other crops, looking through old records leads me principally to a sense of how little we know about causes. Each year is a great one for some crop and a miserable one for some other, with others turning in an about-average performance. The reasons why sweetcorn was good last year and runner beans useless (at least in my garden), made good talking-points over the fence, but they remain as elusive as ever. Certainly little emerges that is concrete enough to act on.

My resolution for 1980 – indeed for the whole of the '80s – is to label everything properly. Properly means permanently. After years of experiment I have settled for names punched on a strip of lead, of the thickness used for roofing. The lead cuts easily with shears to whatever size the length of the name demands. The letters are punched on one at a time, but with a bit of practice it goes remarkably quickly. I always add the date, and sometimes the provenance of the plant. Next year's resolution will be to add a code-number relating the plant to a card-index file with all the details.

—*February*—

FRAGILE BEAUTY

I recently reported the death last year of Donna Lelia Caetani, whose garden at Ninfa, near Rome, is one of the magic places of earth. I was pessimistic about the future of the garden but can now report that a trust has been formed to maintain it.

The great question is whether a garden can successfully be kept in character without either its creator or at least the sort of expertise Britain possesses in the National Trust. It is a highly topical question. The ultimate fate of the Hanbury gardens at La Mortola, recently much in the news, and also of the Villa Taranto on Lake Maggiore, depends on the quality of the advice available now that the influence of their makers has gone.

All three gardens were Anglo-Italian creations. Their special quality comes from a fusion of Italian elements of design (and climate) with a love of plants almost unknown in Italy. It is very doubtful whether Italian officialdom, however well-intentioned, could keep such subtle and complex creations in being. At worst they could become like the Villa d'Este, whose famous garden of fountains is a disgrace. I called there, too, on my visit to Rome. Although I had been warned to expect the worst I was appalled. Squalid is the only word for its state of abandonment, overgrowth and decay, in horrific combination with hordes of litter-crazy tourists.

A MONSTROUS VEGETABLE

I came across the following intriguing reference in *Le Bon Jardinier*, by A. Boileau and E. Vilmorin, of the year 1843. 'The tomato can very successfully be grafted on to the potato, using the herbaceous graft *à la Tschudy*. The result is a crop of potatoes underground, and a crop of tomatoes above.'

Is this a forgotten art? Was it a gimmick that didn't really work? Or am I the only person who doesn't grow pomatoes? It would be amusing if someone produced a demonstration plant – perhaps at a show this summer.

—*March*—

IN FOR TEN PENNIES

On 2 January, the famous penny entrance fee at Kew Gardens went up to 10 pence – still, heaven knows, a bargain price for a visit to the most fascinating of all gardens. The Government's determination not to go on spending more and more of our money has necessarily made the Royal Botanical Gardens rein in some of its activities, both behind the scenes in research and in full public view. In token whereof it has been decided to cancel this year's Open Days in the first week of May. Normally on these three days the herbarium and laboratories are open to educational institutions, or indeed anyone who applies in advance for a ticket.

—May—

PLANTS NEED AIR

Do you ever wonder if the BBC gives gardening and its possibilities for broadcasting any thought at all?

Statistically, being the nation's number one pastime, it deserves at least as much time as any sport. True it lacks the drama and news-worthiness of Test Matches and Cup Ties. But when Radio 3 is turned over interminably to the reminiscences of ex-bowlers, punctuated by the occasional smack of the willow, I ponder longingly on how much more interesting and fruitful it would be to give the mike to some of our senior gardeners – or even some of our junior ones.

Of course we all listen to 'Gardener's Question Time' – don't we? The other day I heard them seriously discussing, of all absurd topics, the urgency of getting snow off your lawn. (It can apparently cause fungus problems.) I spent a happy few moments debating where I would put the stuff (concluding that the kettle would be the best place) before I turned off the radio with a snort and a resolve to write a paragraph demanding more and better gardening on the air.

—June—

HALCYON DAYS

An unseasonal month like February is a good test of whether you are a sensuous or a neurotic gardener. Were you able to bask in those still clear days, when you could dibble away in warm corners in your shirt-sleeves, with no thought save for the crocuses and aconites and snowdrops and scillas and even early daffodils and anemones wide open in the sun? Or were the halcyon days spoilt for you by thoughts of all that premature growth being clobbered by the frosts to come?

I made a cursory count on Leap Day and collected 39 kinds of flowers – counting the willows, birches and alders as one – or rather three; and the same for the irises, crocuses and hellebores.

If anything is tending to turn me neurotic at the moment it is the loathsome coral spot fungus, which far from confining itself to dead wood and odd snags, as it should if it read the text books, dashes about the garden seeking to liberate the souls of trees and shrubs of every description. Maples it seems especially to like – or should I say dislike? But it came as a shock the other day when a grand old choisya suddenly looked mortally sick, its wood covered with red dots.

FOR POSTERITY

Perhaps the most notable memory of last year was meeting the new-born arboretum at Castle Howard. The age of enterprise on a lordly scale is not dead so long as people like George Howard and his resident plantsman, Jim Russell, can devise and plant 70 acres of new arboretum, with some 3,000 trees, in one winter – and such a winter as last year's.

The soil in the shallow valleys surrounding the ridge where Castle Howard stands is notably fertile. Though rainfall is low, the wind persistent and the winter long and cold, trees have grown splendidly here since the original planting of Vanbrugh's time.

Vanbrugh must be smiling to himself to see a new plan on his sort of scale. No one, except possibly the planters, looking at the acres of saplings, can even guess what the effect will be in a hundred years' time. For that matter no one has seen a whole new landscape planted on such a scale for almost a hundred years.

—*August*—

PARADISE LOST

How many visitors to Wisley, going down the Portsmouth Road, have any idea that within three miles of the garden they pass one of the most fascinating and romantic ruined landscape gardens in the country? The haunted-looking brick tower above the road to the left, accoutred in the banality of electricity pylons, is one of the follies of Painshill, an eighteenth-century estate on the scale of Stourhead, now utterly forlorn and overgrown, visited only by fishermen who come to fish its vast lake.

The great iron pumping-wheel that brought up water from the River Mole, the summer-houses and sham castle and Chinese bridge and bathing pool (now dwarfed by the biggest cedar of Lebanon I have ever seen) would be enough to make it nationally important. But its grotto is in a class by itself – chamber after chamber, with a canal running through the middle, all clad in grotesque rocks and lined with sparkling felspar. I'm not sure that there is another like it outside of Xanadu. Though it was damaged in the last war it is not beyond repair.

The local Elmbridge Council has been making moves to save it for some years without managing to clinch the deal. This surely is what the Land Fund is for. It could not find a more quintessentially English, a more lost and yet more convenient part of our heritage.

—September—

THE RISK OF OAK WILT

Those who are still worried about the danger of oak wilt spreading to this country, despite the reassurances of the Forestry Commission, had an opportunity in June to question Forestry Commission officials about the risks at a seminar organized by the Tree Council.

Dr Gibbs of the Forestry Commission gave an admirable account of the disease, which he said is very like Dutch elm disease in its mode of operation, though at present more selective in its prey. In North America it is rapidly fatal to red oaks (*Quercus rubra* and *Q. coccinea* are the most frequently met of this group here) but only disfiguring to white oaks (the group that includes our *Q. robur* and *Q. petraea*).

Whereas elm disease spreads like wild-fire, the fungus carried from tree to tree by feeding bark beetles, oak wilt spreads only slowly, and that largely by contact between roots, for lack of an efficient insect vector in North America.

The frightening possibility is that a European insect could easily provide the transport it needs and decimate American oaks, if it were to find its way over the Atlantic – or that the wilt, if it were introduced here at all, could fall into the wrong insects' hands and spread as catastrophically as elm disease.

The Forestry Commission's control measures are the banning of American oak imports with bark on and the compulsory drying or sterilizing of timber with sapwood (in which the fungus could survive). The Scotch Whisky industry is the principal user of American oak, most of it in the form of second-hand Bourbon barrels from Kentucky. But many loads of planks are also shipped, and these are always liable to contain a small amount of bark. For this reason the Commission maintains a force of 157 part-time inspectors, 80 of them at the ports, to do spot-checks on timber shipments reported to them by the Customs. When they find bark they have it destroyed.

But this is the weak link in our defences. Although it is very unlikely that timber from a diseased tree will turn up here as planks there is no guarantee, only a possibility, that if it did the container would be opened and inspected. If the improbable should happen, and the right insect find the infected planks, our oaks would be at serious risk. The Forestry Commission put the chance at one in many millions. Having heard their case my impression is that the odds are shorter than they claim.

—October—

'AMPLE CHOICE'

I was horrified to read in an article by Roy Hay that a dozen varieties of flowering cherry and rhododendron is 'ample choice' for him or anyone else. Surely this is encouraging the very pestilence that has swept through our nurseries and garden centres, the curse of 'rationalization' that threatens the very existence of unusual or rare plants. We are told that it is only economically possible to propagate plants with an established demand – or 'exciting novelties'.

Gardening journalists compound the problem by limiting their recommendations to plants that their readers will be able to find without trouble. They should be doing exactly the opposite and opening gardeners' eyes to the marvellous variety of plants that only a few dedicated nurserymen offer.

—November—

INSPIRATIONS AT THE SHOWS

The peculiar value and interest of the monthly RHS shows at Vincent Square, as opposed to Chelsea, is that they reflect exactly the horticultural moment. The relatively limited range of plants, with nothing (or not much) forced or held back, allows you to compare the actual state of your garden with what is on show. If there is a better form of something you are growing the comparison is made easy and immediate. If you are looking for a plant of a particular height or colour to improve a border at that particular moment of the year you may well find it then and there – a more exact and satisfactory way of choosing plants than trying to carry your desiderata in your head until the catalogues come round.

These thoughts struck me as I admired the herbacious specialist Carlile's summer-border flowers in August and decided that a lively violet bergamot would be better than the common red 'Cambridge Scarlet' in a border with phlox and daylilies. The pace is gentle enough at monthly shows, particularly on the second day, to make such momentous calculations in tranquillity.

HORTUS NANA

Garden-visiting this year has brought me face-to-face on several occasions with outbreaks of dwarf conifers where they have no business. Isolation is essential to them. Divorced from other forms of gardening they can be curiously effective – Bedgebury through the wrong end of a telescope. In their now-conventional association with heathers they betray the yearning of *homo hortensis* for the wildness of the moors.

But I have seen beds of dwarfs in juxtaposition with sumptuous summer borders, with laden fruit-trees and with cascading roses. I am afraid instead of painting an acceptable garden picture it just makes them look the sterile freaks of nature they really are.

—December—

Wish You Were Here

It was the fulfilment of a long-cherished ambition to go to the Alps at the end of August and scramble around at the receding snow-line on the Mont Blanc massif, at 7,000 feet or so, among the carpets of spring flowers.

However much one reads about alpines, I at least had never adequately imagined so many plants associated in gardeners' minds with rockeries, if not pans in alpine houses, spreading in their millions across mile after mile of mountain. It is wonderful how they change with the terrain from one minute to the next where the unseen rock below the soil suddenly plunges deep, or is shallow and dry, or thin but soaked by a hidden spring. How the rocks themselves are seldom so smooth that some seed will not lodge and life begin: a pad of androsace blunts a crag; a tangle of juniper smothers a boulder. Tiny soldanellas and Bavarian gentians of intense sapphire are already in flower while the ground is still raw and desolate, the herbs yellow, within days of the snow melting. Bright lilac pansies choose to combine with flaming hawkweeds and dark-leaved trailing willows to mingle on the brink of streams with pale ferns.

I had the perfect mentor for such a first visit: Correvon's *La Flore Alpine* of 1911, illustrated with the paintings of Philippe Robert. I would not go quite so far as Correvon, who compares the artist with Fra Angelico. His painting is frankly decorative, with a broad hint of art nouveau, yet somehow fresher and easier to follow than any more 'naturalistic' illustration – and far more instructive than handbooks using photographs. Correvon is no dry botanist either; he quotes poetry – the least one can do in the presence of such beauty – and tells charming stories.

Travelling home through eastern France and the Black Forest, I began to wonder if we are not a little too smug in considering ourselves the great nation of gardeners. Perhaps we pride ourselves too much on the achievements of the rich amateurs who have created our great gardens, but forget that others do everyday small-scale gardening at least as well as we do, and often very much better.

There are villages in Alsace and the Black Forest where the gardens and balconies and window-boxes are so dressed with flowers that you would think the Queen was coming. There is a generosity, not to mention skill and care and pride, in continental summer bedding which is rarely seen in this country. Our front gardens of roses, lovely as they can be, must appear to be the lazy way to a spot of colour in the eyes of visitors from such flower-decked regions.

ON YOUR MARKS

When the immensely popular new 'golden' version of the now-universal Leyland cypress was launched in 1975 I thought it would be rather fun to have a tree race.

I bought a number of plants of 'Castlewellan' from Pennell's of Lincoln, who introduced it, and distributed them among friends round the country. I also planted four or five in different parts of my own garden. Though not as gold as the brightest Lawsons or macro-carpas it is a pleasing colour, and rather more dense and fluffy than its green counterparts – corresponding, presumably, to its supposedly slower growth.

The results of the race have no scientific value whatever, since the soils and sites vary widely and none of the recipients was obliged either to feed and water or to desist from so doing. But it is still quite amusing to note that the best of the trees at home in Essex is 19 feet high, in a dampish and sheltered spot with little competition. A group of trees in close company with a beech tree, a greedy beast, are 17 feet plus. One in East Sussex, on well-drained sandy clay with little shelter (and I guess not watered) is also 17 feet. One in north Kent on exposed downland chalk, watered only in its first year, 10 feet. And one in a well-sheltered site on limy clay in Gloucestershire is 10 feet plus – not bad considering that, true gardener that she is, its proprietor has moved it at least twice.

Altogether an alarmingly fast tree.

CUNCTA·SIMUL
FIERI·VETAT
IRREVOCABILIS·
·············HORA

1981

—*January*—

THE ERRORS OF THE SPRING

I wonder how many gardeners know Marvell's lovely ode 'To Little T.C. in a Prospect of Flowers', in which he imagines that this little girl can charm flowers into having qualities they lack. He tells her to:

> Reform the errors of the spring.
> Make that the tulip may have share
> Of sweetness, seeing she is fair,
> And roses of their thorns disarm.
> But most, procure
> That violets may a longer age endure.

A sweet-scented tulip is a lovely idea. I am sure that all gardeners have dreams of plants they would love to see conjured into existence. Blue roses are an obvious example, but this is crying for the moon. I really mean simple improvements which one might reasonably hope to find in a seed-bed.

The plant I long for is a white-flowered laburnum. How fresh and elegant those tassels would be; how they would stand out among dark trees, and hang like ghostly wraiths in the dusk if they were white. I have a 'golden-leaved' form of laburnum that has its moment, when flowers and leaves are almost the same colour, but the moment soon passes, leaving a faintly ill-looking tree for the summer. A sterile laburnum that formed no seedpods at all is another chore for Little T.C.

PUBLIC SHRUBS

The town of Troyes, east of Paris, has one of France's most extensive medieval quarters, happily in a splendid state of preservation. A large part of it is a pedestrian precinct. But its cobbles are cluttered, its quaintly tilting corners sullied by the intrusive beastliness of concrete 'planters' filled with the predictable public gardeners' assortment of indestructible shrubs. The dreariness of a jumble of mahonia, cotoneaster, berberis and the rest, struggling to exist on a draughty corner under a mulch of sweet wrappers and soft-drink cans needs no describing. But it would scarcely be better if it were well-chosen and well-kept seasonal bedding. The streets themselves have so much character that plants are merely an intrusion.

Troyes is typical of scores of towns, in this country too, with plants where no plants should be. It is a common misapprehension among public authorities that any and all corners of town, suburb and country are better for a spot of horticulture. Dotting shrubs along streets is all too often a negation of gardening.

— *March* —

CRYSTAL BALL

Should gardening be taught in schools? Why not? Cookery and carpentry are. Gardening takes you much further into the natural causes of things than either. And coming generations, freed by the silicon chip from the privilege of working for a living, are going to have long lives of leisure that will desperately need such a point of contact with reality.

Gardening as a serious craft, up to a high standard of perfection, could be one of the best ways of filling the time that runs a risk of being perilously, possibly destructively, empty.

There is, or ought to be, a direct connection between unwanted leisure and the creation, and maintenance, of wonderful gardens.

Big gardens with the richness of detail that needs dedicated hand labour (rather than mere machinery) have become impracticable. The price of labour puts much craftsmanship out of reach even of public authorities. At the same time armies of the jobless are deprived of the satisfaction they could find in gardening for want of anyone who could afford their wages.

It is part of a complex problem. There may never again be enough 'productive' jobs in the old sense to go round all the energetic and creative members of society. Eventually we will have to redefine the concepts of 'work' and 'a job'. If someone provides me with an opportunity for doing something I enjoy, should he have to pay me for doing it as well?... if the alternative is not having it done at all?

Job-creation programmes begin to nibble at the issue. But they are merely tinkering, not facing the dilemma squarely. One of the principal problems is the spectre of exploitation, which is a difficult one to lay. If there is a private owner (rather than a company or a public institution) in the picture it is joined by the spectre of personal service – which makes it harder still.

These musings appear in this column because they are central to the future of horticulture. Millions of little one-man gardens do not add up to the equal of the great gardens of our past. Nor do our publicly owned gardens, however diligently they are run.

Somehow we must find a way of harnessing the nation's green fingers. It will have to be by co-operation out of goodwill.

– April –

TERMINAL 1 AT WISLEY

There are now probably few Members of the Society who are still unaware of the very serious threat to Wisley posed by the quite unexpected proposal to re-open Wisley Airfield as a businessmens' airport to handle 30,000 flights a year.

In fact there were probably few Members who even realized that there was an airfield next door to Wisley. It was closed at the end of the war (except for occasional test flights which ceased in 1972), and undertakings were given in writing that the runway would be taken up and the land returned to its pre-war use, which was farming.

Suddenly in 1979, out of the blue, came an application from an unknown little company, Jenstate Ltd, to put it to the much more profitable use of catering for executive jets. Planning permission was, not unexpectedly, refused. Jenstate appealed against the refusal. Meanwhile, last summer, while the appeal was pending, the government's Property Services Agency sold the land, complete with runway, back to its pre-war owner, Lord Lytton. The sale went through with almost unseemly speed; I am told the deed was done within 24 hours.

There was a terrific rumpus in the House of Lords when our President (among others) told the tale. Comparisons were made with the government's notorious breach of faith over Crichel Down.

Lord Lytton is an octogenarian peer with residences in Somerset and Sussex, who describes his recreation (in *Who's Who*) as 'reclaiming two lakes'. It appears he intends to add one airport to his bag.

HORTUS PICTUS

There is rarely a shortage of talented flower painters. But hardly anyone it seems these days paints gardens. I always look out for garden paintings at the Royal Academy Summer Exhibition. Several painters show a feeling for gardens; they crop up as views through windows, or incidentally in a composition with some other intention.

What is missing is the studied garden portrait which was one of the glories of Edwardian times. At its best, in the masterly watercolours of George Elgood (who illustrated several of Gertrude Jekyll's books) or Margaret Waterfield, it provided the most sensitive portrayal of garden beauty that has ever been achieved.

No photographer has been able to embody so much of the intention of the gardener as Margaret Waterfield, for example, in what she modestly called her 'colour sketches'. The photographer must always single out and focus on some bold and substantial feature to enable his customer (client? consumer?) to get his bearings. In practice the photographer nearly always chooses a piece of architecture or a statue or even just the reassuring perspective of a path.

But the painter has no such restraints. He can make light do the work of selection and editing. The composition of the painting itself can provide all the architecture he needs. There may be other elements there besides, but the painter is not obliged to put in anything that would distract attention from his theme.

—June—

ANOTHER WORLD

Tradescant is lucky enough to see quite a bit of the world on one pretext or another, but very rarely has he been so thrilled as with Kirstenbosch in autumn this spring.

Kirstenbosch is the botanical garden of the Cape, which climbs the back of Table Mountain up to the point where the sheer rock begins. The garden is a little epitome of the history, as well as the botany, of the Cape. The colossal hedge of thorny shrubs planted in 1660 as the limit of the first colony rolls like a great breaker of vegetation through the grounds. In one ferny dingle a lovely little brick-lined, spring-fed bath recalls by its shape the name of its eighteenth-century builder, and presumably bather, Colonel Bird.

Below it the stream runs in a bed ingeniously paved with flat stones so as to be both stream and path at once – a deliciously cooling compromise where the temperature is often in the 90s. Its shady banks, here stiff with clivias, there strewn with streptocarpus, emerge into the sunlight through a grove of tree-ferns, then an orchard of gardenias, like orange trees bearing both fragrant white flowers and fat fruit together – only the fruit of the gardenia is a pale grey sausage.

Further down a peculiar pale grey aralia, *Cussonia paniculata*, shakes fistfuls of chalky deep-lobed leaves above the great cabbagy hearts of the cycads. On the dry slopes above more cycads, equipped with fiercer and fiercer spikes, give way to endless ericas, proteas in protean variety and to the tinsel glitter of the extraordinary silver trees. Imagine the satin silveriness of the palest cricket-bat willow in a tree designed by the same primitive engineer as the monkey-puzzle. Where the ground is barest and most arid between these warrior-like plants suddenly up pops a blushing amaryllis, as frail as flesh.

Extraordinary as it seems in a country with such a sensational flora most South-African gardeners seem to look towards Europe for their plants. In a local nursery I saw only rows of birches, hawthorns, poplars, cypresses, Australian gums and New Zealand flax.

Kirstenbosch is grandly and proudly South African. I can't wait to go back.

POSTUME, POSTUME

There is a long tradition of inscribing witty or sentimental thoughts on sundials. I suppose the best-known is 'I only count the sunny hours'. A friend in San Francisco has sent me a graffito (the speciality of that breezy city) that beats the lot. 'Time', it says, 'is nature's way of stopping everything from happening at once.'

Please can someone translate it for me into Latin (Ciceronian, not botanical) so that I can leave a little reward for the learned when they walk round my garden?

Or produce a better one?

—July—

MORE FROM THE CÔTE D'AZUR

A visit to La Mortola in April did nothing to encourage hope that this great garden's troubles are over. The lovely promontory, with the Mediterranean breaking at its foot, is in a limbo of bureaucratic shadow-boxing. I was told that the document transferring its control from a ministry in Rome to the Rector of Genoa University is now in its seventh draft form. And meanwhile the weeds grow, the trees topple and the great collection of exotics goes uncatalogued and uncared for. Money, apparently, is available for 'extraordinary' purposes only. In other words you can have a new sprinkler system but no fertilizers. The gardeners are not insured for tree work – and are not paid any too regularly in any case.

It was heartening, in contrast, to see the brave and thorough way the French forestry authorities are renewing the seriously overgrown garden at the Villa Thuret along the coast on Cap d'Antibes, clearing out large sections where honey-fungus has taken hold, to deep plough and fumigate the ground. And it was nothing less than astonishing to visit, all too briefly, the great private botanical garden at Les Cèdres, created by the late Monsieur Marnier-Lapostolle on Cap Ferrat and now looked after by his widow.

From broad parterres of succulents (many of them roofed-over for the winter even in that climate) to thick groves of giant bamboos shutting out the sunlight, it is an unimaginable collection; a vegetable wonderland and a tantalizing model for what La Mortola could be.

—September—

I ONLY COUNT...

There are some odd sundials about. Following my challenge to translate (or beat) my Californian entry I have been offered several. The most unsunny must be the lugubriously inscribed '*Toutes les heures blessent; la dernière tue*' – Every hour wounds; the last hour kills.

On a brighter, triter note a friend in Somerset sent me '*Sine Sole Sileo*', which I dare to translate as 'No sun, I am mum', or for prettier gardens shall we say 'The sun obscur'd, I hold my peace?' As he dazzlingly added, isn't that a grand helio-trope?

NICETURTIUMS

Victorian gardening books sometimes whet our appetites for flowers that have disappeared without trace (which is, of course, the *raison d'être* of the National Council for the Conservation of Gardens – but more of that anon).

A neighbour drew my attention to *Familiar Garden Flowers*, circa 1908, by Shirley Hibberd and Edward Hulme, which praises the white, and even the purple, nasturtiums which were shown at the Paris Exhibition of 1878.

I love the thought of pure white nasturtiums. How cool they would be, with their salady green leaves and succulent stems, finding enough moisture in the dust bowl of a rooty bank to make pale moony eyes at you in the dusk. France is presumably the place to look for them – but I fear the French are even more careless about mislaying their plants than we are.

—October—

WHERE THERE'S LIFE

I have been finding our few remaining elm trees almost unbearably beautiful this summer; the apparent certainty of their death makes their strength and grace too poignant for pleasure. So I heard with real excitement the report of a seminar at Salford University which challenges the resignation we have all been feeling.

There are two new factors to rekindle hope. The first chiefly concerns the North, where the disease is still merely sporadic. It appears that the latitude, with a shorter growing season, hampers the breeding of the beetles that carry the disease. This fact, combined with the relative scarcity of the most vulnerable species, the field elm, suggests that a true epidemic is less likely north of the Mersey-Humber line.

The second is the development of a means of trapping the beetles in their multitudes. American experiments have been successful in isolating the chemical substance that attracts the beetles to the trees (and each other). Sticky traps baited with it have killed millions.

But the new technique is to inject a diseased elm with a substance that kills it rapidly. As it dies it produces the attractive 'pheromone' in lavish quantities and beetles pour in from miles around to breed in the bark. The tree is then cut down and burnt, and all the larvae with it.

The Salford seminar produced figures that should leave our public authorities in no doubt at all. The cost of an effective sanitation campaign (i.e. felling and burning immediately wherever the disease appears) will probably be about one-third of the final cost of letting the disease run its course.

Elbow Room

I wonder what I'm doing wrong. The magic of wallflowers (apart from their wonderful smell, on the winy side of violets) was that they grew on walls. You didn't plant them there, but an old wall acquired plants that lasted for years, hanging on like a dinghy sailor in a squall but giving their adopted home that wonderful seal of approval that only self-sown plants can give.

Or plants that layer themselves. A bough of a tree that has felt so comfortable with its elbow resting on the ground that is has taken root like the mark of a mature – even a serene – garden. I'm happy to report that the walnut tree by the back here has declared itself satisfied by shooting up vigorously from where a branch has drooped down to the daffodils.

—November—

Conservation – A New Angle

Since last winter I have been beginning to learn the delights and perils of having a conservatory. It could hardly have been a better summer for a beginner: wet enough to keep me in it a lot of the time, and cool enough for some plants which, I soon realized, would otherwise be scorched to a cinder.

The speed of growth of most things is quite intoxicating. My potted olive tree, bought at a Vincent Square show in the spring, is already three times the size it was. A strawberry vine with pale rather round leaves is 10 feet high and as for plumbago, a cutting a year ago, I can only say I am relieved it is in a pot. In a bed it would have swallowed the house by now.

We decided rightly or wrongly to grow everything in pots – mainly, I confess, so that we can rapidly recover from any disasters by keeping alternatives in the greenhouse. So far nothing has gone that wrong, but I can see the merit of keeping, say, some of the winter-flowering Australian acacias tucked away until their moment of glory is due.

I will report back from time to time on how we get on.

I Only Count...

I am vastly impressed by the scholarship of my readers. In June I mentioned the motto for a sundial that a friend in San Francisco had sent me, and asked for a Latin translation. No less than a score of very passable versions arrived on my desk.

Wanting to do justice to such sterling effort I asked Theo Zinn, Senior Classics master at Westminster School, to be the judge.

He tells me that the standard was high enough to make it a close run thing, but in the end he chose an entrant who put in three different versions, in the styles of Virgil, Ovid and Catullus. He is Mr Brian Kay, of Pond Cottage, Botolph Claydon, Buckinghamshire.

The original ran, if you remember, 'Time is nature's way of stopping everything from happening at once.'

It is put most neatly in a Virgilian hexameter:

CUNCTA SIMUL FIERI VETAT IRREVOCABILIS HORA.

For larger sundials, however, there is something to be said for the more deliberate Ovidian couplet:

CUR NATURA DIEM BIS SEX DIVISIT IN HORAS?
NE FIANT UNO TEMPORE CUNCTA REOR.

A very slight hiccup in the hendecasyllables à la Catullus prevented, Mr Zinn says, a perfect hat trick. Congratulations, Mr Kay, and thank you to all the Latinists who sent me versions.

1982

—January—

MAN BITES DOGMA

Gardeners have long been resigned to the apparent arrogance of botanists in suddenly changing the names of well-known plants. However many times the rules of nomenclature are explained to us we feel affronted when *Viburnum fragrans*, so simply and appropriately named, suddenly becomes *Viburnum farreri*, or *Rosa rubrifolia* turns its coat and has to be called *Rosa glauca*.

But now there is a glimmer of hope of a less draconian application of the rules in future. British members returning from the nomenclatural sessions of the International Botanical Congress in Sydney last year reported that at last the conservative rump had been outvoted.

The issue was wheat. If the rules were to be applied in their full rigour the botanical name of wheat would change from *Triticum aestivum* to *T. hibernum* – from summer, in fact, to winter. The forces of reason protested. How could the vast trouble and expense of renaming one of the world's most important crops be justified by a pedantic quibble? And they won. A new clause was written into the rules. From now on if the congress decides that a species has sufficient economic importance it may declare its established name sacrosanct.

It remains to be seen how future meetings interpret the new clause. The Director of Wisley, one of those responsible for the victory of reason over dogma, thinks that under the new rule *Viburnum fragrans* might well have been able to keep its popular name.

NUNC SILEO

My kind correspondents have now equipped me with enough sundial mottoes to go into business...What business?

Hilaire Belloc wrote the clincher:

I am a sundial, and I make a botch
Of what is done much better by a watch.

—*February*—

NEWS FROM KEW

The Director of Kew, Professor Arthur Bell, works in one of the most practical and vital areas of botany: enlarging the range of foodstuffs that mankind can eat without poisoning himself. He is a biochemist turned botanist who specializes in toxicity, which many plants have developed to protect themselves from predators. If toxic levels can be reduced genetically a number of plants that are now poisonous could become excellent sources of nourishment.

Lathyrus sativus, for example, is a rich source of protein in poor areas of India, but a regular diet of it paralyzes the legs irreversibly. Breed it without the toxin, and a huge human problem disappears.

Since Sir Joseph Banks sent Bligh to introduce breadfruit to the West Indies, Kew has been deeply concerned with the practical uses of plants. Professor Bell belongs to this tradition. As to the gardens, he loves them, he says, 'as millions do'.

— *March* —

THROUGH THE LOOKING-GLASS

Regulars will remember the alternating hope and frustration of my commentary on the fate of the Giardino Botanico Hanbury at La Mortola, on its spectacular promontory just where Italy meets France.

Last autumn frustration was giving way to anger. Twelve months after the conference at the garden at which the Directors of Kew and Wisley had been assured of imminent consultations and speedy action nothing whatever had been done, and the garden had sunk deeper than ever into dereliction.

Italian bureaucracy is clearly prepared to make no concessions to mere reality. A pine lies where it fell last spring because there is no petrol for the chainsaw, which doesn't work anyway, and in any case the gardeners are not insured for tree work. The pergola is collapsing. The herbarium has been locked for years, accessible only to the mice that are eating the specimens. Plants are regularly plundered by the unsupervized public. There is no heating for the greenhouses. New reservoirs have been installed, under the direction of an architect who held no consultation with the director. He also put in hydrants. But there are no pipes between the two.

I even learned recently that the 'new regime' requires the gardeners to become civil servants, which most of them are debarred from doing since they are over 35, the maximum age for entry.

On my next visit I expect to see a pack of playing cards playing croquet with flamingoes.

It is not fair to Italy, though, to suggest that it has a monopoly of complacency over important gardens. I was recently told another appalling tale by Elizabeth McClintock, one of California's most respected plantswomen and a member of the board of the Strybing Arboretum in San Francisco's famous Golden Gate Park.

The park is a block of 1,000 acres on very sandy soil starting by the Pacific and extending like a long tongue (about three miles long) into the heart of San Francisco. When it was laid out early in the century the essential first planting was a deep windbreak, chiefly of pines and cypresses, to seaward, repeated several times to divide the park into sheltered areas for planting a huge collection of trees and other plants.

The windbreaks are now over mature and cracking up. Once the defences are down the ocean blast will destroy the rest of the park (including the Strybing Arboretum) in a year or two. San Francisco's celebrated and dynamic mayor Diane Feinstein was told that funds were needed for a hefty replanting. She even paid the park a visit. Putting the telescope to her blind eye, she said, 'It's lovely. What a lot of beautiful trees we have.'

Are there still no votes for politicians in trees and parks – even in San Francisco?

– April –

THE ROSE AND THE VINE

In any fanciful hierarchy of plants for the sheer pleasure they give there are two that must surely intertwine in a place above all others – the rose and the vine.

If this were Tennyson's Diary or indeed Sir Alma Tadema's instead of your earthy correspondent Trad's, you could expect a relentless profusion of tender buds and ripening clusters, twining tendrils and blown petals on the grass.

It was a recent visit to Bordeaux that made me think about the two together. By tradition every vine row in the Bordeaux vineyards has a red rose planted by the stake at the end. It is nearly always the same small red rose, propagated by cuttings by the wine grower. I've never discovered its name, but its colour is like a promise of claret to come, and I'm told it has a valuable practical use; it is just a shade more subject to mildew than the vines. When there are signs of mildew on the rose it is time to get out and spray the vineyard.

Strange to say there are parts of the Médoc where the wine is excellent but the soil is too heavy for even roses to thrive. I brought back a soil sample from Château Loudenne to Wisley for analysis and was asked if I'd got it from the moon; they had never seen any soil so leaden and devoid of humus.

The old-fashioned roses I planted in a long border at Loudenne, overlooking the vines and a marvellous sweeping view of the Gironde, there 10 miles wide, have just sulked, despite wagonloads of good farmyard stuff.

At another château, Grand-Puy-Lacoste in Pauillac, where the soil is more open and gravelly, there are the relics of a collection of old roses in a dream-like *jardin potager*, among vegetables and cutting flowers in alternating rows. I brought home a strange fragrant deep violet rambler, centred and streaked with white, which I had never seen before. Roland the gardener called it 'Blaye', from the town across the estuary where he had got it. I had decided to call it 'Grand-Puy-Lacoste' when I recognized its description in Graham Thomas's *Climbing Roses Old and New*. It is 'Veilchenblau' – not nearly such a pretty name. I've given it a vine for company, to remind it of home.

Snow on Snow

We had an ample demonstration last December of the immense destructive power of snow under certain conditions. Wisley was badly hit, particularly in the pinetum, where pines and cedars were split and torn, many past repairing. A big *Liquidambar orientalis* was uprooted by the weight of snow in its branches. Kew reported a great holm oak collapsed and almost every cedar losing at least one of its horizontal branches. At Wakehurst, a score of big old rhododendrons standing in wet ground keeled over and hollies, normally pliant and good snow resisters, were torn apart.

The damage was mainly to evergreens because they collect most snow and so carry most weight. The ground and the trees were already rain-sodden when the snow started. As it fell the temperature fell too. At Kew, Charles Erskine, in charge of the arboretum, told me they went out first thing to knock the snow off the branches but it was too late; it had already frozen on. More snow fell and the combined weight of ice and snow was crushing. And that was before the night of the blizzard on 12 December.

We usually lead such a mild and sheltered life on these islands that we have little idea of the strains and stresses of a real continental or New England winter. It is a wonder that their parks and gardens have any big trees intact at all.

—*July*—

THE UNQUALIFIED CONSERVATORY

I promised an occasional report from our recently acquired conservatory. The great consolation of last winter was the steadfast tolerance by its plants of very chilly conditions, with the maximum daytime temperature around 40°F for days and at one time two weeks on end, and a recorded minimum of 35°F. The only casualty was an arborescent poinsettia which I stupidly overwatered. Everything else looked at least healthy, and two or three plants showed their scorn of the cold (or perhaps their gratitude for a kilowatt or two) by flowering all winter long. Of these the star was *Salvia coerulea*, an acquisition from the conservatory at Knightshayes with searching purple flowers that set off the indefatigable yellow wands of *Mahonia lomariifolia*. More quietly, the pale pink *Lavatera bicolor* got its seasons completely inside out and flowered from December to April.

By the end of March the limelight had shifted to a great pot of arum lilies, a present from a generous neighbour, which put up a score of sumptuous flowers, to azaleas whose names I better not even try to get right and to *Rhododendron iteophyllum* whose white, just-blushing flowers have aristocracy etched into every feature and into their feminine – dare I say sexy? – scent.

With April came a glorious fuzz of lilac all over the Australian mint bush, *Prostanthera rotundifolia,* the first red passion flowers, geraniums starting up – not that some of them ever stopped – the heavenly sweet white *Buddleja asiatica,* the orange *Clivia* from the Cape, and the triumphant scarlet of the Chilean *Mitraria coccinea.*

There is no clever stuff with colour schemes here; there seems to be enough green to take care of all this motley collection. It is strange, though, that there aren't more books about gardening under glass like this; it's the best fun I ever had.

DARWIN'S HOME GROUND

The centenary of the death of Charles Darwin was in April. For 40 years he lived at Downe in Kent, only 16 miles from London, where the Kent Trust for Nature Conservation preserves the bank on which he studied – among other things – orchids. To celebrate the centenary they have bought the adjoining bluebell wood and are appealing for funds for the purchase.

We are so used to the idea of Darwin the traveller and images of the *Beagle* and the Galapagos Islands that we overlook his quieter work with our native flora. The North Downs were as important to the progression of his ideas as the South Seas. In a charming article in the *Kent Trust's Journal* the wardens of the Orchis Bank Reserve quote Darwin on just such a spot: 'It is interesting to contemplate a tangled bank, clothed with plants of many kinds, with birds singing in the bushes, with various insects flitting about and with worms crawling through the damp earth, and to recall that these elaborately constructed forms, so different from each other, and so dependent on each other in so complex a manner, have all been produced by laws acting around us.'

Poor old Darwin. The church he offended with his theory of evolution saw to it that he was not honoured by his country. But could he want a better memorial than 22 acres of the North Downs with its marvellously varied flora, perpetually flourishing as he remembers it?

—*August*—

NO NUT, THIS ONE

We had the bracing experience of an unfamiliar genius in our midst in the spring. Brazil's great landscaper-botanist, Roberto Burle Marx, came to give lectures at Kew and the Royal College of Art. I sat on the floor in the packed lecture room of the College (others were less lucky; they were standing in the doorways and even the corridors) to hear him expound on half-a-century of exploring and designing in a country most of us know little about.

For one man to be both plant collector and landscape gardener is rare enough. When he excels at both, and is a very good painter into the bargain, and all in an exotic land, the brew is intoxicating.

He showed us private gardens like Eden in the hills behind Rio de Janeiro. He showed us the hideous development of Rio itself; his extravaganza of decorating the whole length of the Copacabana beach with mosaics; the strange lurid flowers he has collected in the jungle and the savage things that the Brazilians are doing to it. He is the most powerful exponent of ecology in a country that is playing with fire.

Physically, Marx is like a cross between Albert Schweitzer and Andre Simon. I suspect that the similarities are more than skin deep. At lunch in the country before the lecture, he broke off from a passionate exposition of the perils of clear-felling a rain forest into a beaming smile when he tasted a good glass of wine. Suddenly he was singing – and very well – a drinking song from the Loire.

— *September* —

ROYAL SPRING

Two of the fruitiest days of a fairy-tale spring were specially commissioned by the Royal Weather Department for the respective visits of the Queen to Kew, to open the restored Temperate House, and the Queen Mother to the Savill Garden, to celebrate the 50th anniversary of the Savill Garden by planting a variegated tulip tree.

The Temperate House is one of the glories of a school of architecture I associate more with Monte Carlo or Cannes than Surrey: the

see-through classical, but on a scale and of a quality that makes the
beholder blink and rub his eyes. It is to the very great credit of everybody concerned at Kew and in Whitehall that this sensational building
has been restored with no sign of a penny pinched. Obviously some of
the planting in it on re-opening day still bore the marks of the trowel,
but the small size of some of the plants only served to emphasize the
splendour of the long-term residents, which had been kept going by
ingenious resources without walls or a roof – and through the coldest
winter on record. The great Chilean palm had a wooden tower round
it to support a polythene overcoat into which hot air was pumped all
through those freezing days and nights.

The Queen unveiled a rather sombre memorial slab with obvious
satisfaction. But – a note in passing – will somebody please bring back
the two vast urns that formerly flanked the main entrance steps but are
now missing?

As for the Savill Garden on a hot day in early June – I don't know
where to begin...and anyway there isn't room. It is a masterpiece. Lord
Aberconway briefly and eloquently reminded us of the genius of Sir
Eric Savill and his (and our) good fortune in his Royal patrons. One
marvellous plant there is, in my mind's eye, even more of a memorial
than the variegated tulip tree: the incredible spire of a Serbian spruce
on the bank between the gate and the stream. It was planted in 1932
and should serve as a lesson to Serbian (and all) spruces everywhere.

Not a soul in the illustrious assembly, I noticed, left without buying
all the plants he or she could carry at the garden centre by the gate.
Another admirable facet of the Savill Garden (alas not of Kew): you
can buy bits to take home.

— *October* —

TREE-BROODING

Sherrards of Newbury had a particularly pretty stand at the July show
at Vincent Square. They arranged a first-class collection of deciduous
trees as simply and naturally as a young wood, uncluttered by shrubs
or any other plants. It made me realize that to be anything like a reflec-
tion of the way Trad really spends his time this diary should touch
much more often on tree-brooding.

Tree-brooding is what silvimaniacs like me do when they wander among their own or anyone else's trees with their minds coasting and their senses picking up the details of leaf, twig, bark and bud, catkin and cone, that make trees such an inexhaustible source of pleasure.

I am not talking of anything methodical; no tape measure, labels, notebook or Hillier's *Manual*. I stop to loosen or remove a plastic tie or pull up a weed now and then. I always have my secateurs in their holster. But really I am just letting the trees talk to me.

Some can make such an impression that the moment stays with you for years. I shall never forget my first sight of the great Lucombe oak at Kew in its spruced-up, newly fed glory this spring. The bald word majesty is all I can manage for this great figure from the eighteenth century, shading half a football-pitch worth of lawn with its dark, dense, glossy, high-arching crown. I salute the arboriculturists who restored it to this splendid perfection. How they must have enjoyed themselves up in that great world of wood.

But I really intended to talk about the little garden trees of my own planting; the ones I commune with every day. The eldest is 10 this year: a very smart big-leaved whitebeam which has done more than I could have asked it to do in 20 years. Let nobody tell you that trees are too slow to bother with. I plant them small, look down at them for two years, eyeball to eyeball with them a year, then up at them for the rest of my life. The first years are when you get to know the details; the manner of budding, the colour of the new leaves and the angles of twig and branch. There are serious decisions to be taken in this nursery period. Often two shoots both look equally determined to be the leader. You must size them up and give the lesser one the chop. Oaks are some of the worst trees in this respect: every bud seems to feel an equal right to take over. In shady places I have found they grow straight and well, but when they are in the sun they shoot and jut and lean all over the place.

I have a very long short list of favourite trees of garden size. Let me just mention a handful that are more worthwhile than the standard garden-centre choice. They may not be readily available, but that should not stop you asking – and looking in the small-ads at the back of *The Garden* where the small specialist nurseries make their pitch.

Of the many willows I love, I think the most sensational is the little silver-white willow, *Salix alba argentea*. I am not sure how little because although mine is growing slowly, a friend has a 30-foot specimen on the bank of a pond. The point of this tree is its finely pointed, intensely silver silky leaves, which make it one of the palest of all trees from a distance – more truly silver than the popular but awkward and angular weeping silver pear. It is odd that the weeping form of this pear is the only one commonly offered, because its non-weeping form is much more graceful, if slightly more vigorous.

I have been enchanted this year with the performance of a newcomer to me, a weeping aspen poplar which came as a cutting from Maurice Mason's amazing collection in Norfolk. It is very stoop-ing, rather like Young's excellent weeping birch, and seems to have smaller leaves with even longer leafstalks than normal aspens. It also has masses of puffy purply-pink male catkins in February. Properly trained (this will be the difficult part) it will be a fine textured mound of restless pinky-green foliage quite distinct from any other plant in the garden.

Another discovery (in the painter John Aldridge's garden) is an *Acer negundo* called *violaceum* which masks a suffusion of winey pigment (prominent in the flowers) under a waxy grey bloom.

I knew if I started on trees the page would shrink. One or two more special favourites will have to wait.

—November—

THE ELEVENTH HOUR

The 50th anniversary of a writer's death is often marked by a flurry of 'appreciations' and 'reappraisals'. There is no mystery. His or her published work comes out of copyright and publishers can use the hard-wrought words without the nuisance of having to pay any royalties.

The very last day of this year is the release date for the works of Gertrude Jekyll. Seeing the price that second-hand copies of her books have been fetching no doubt several publishers have been thinking of facsimile or new editions. They will have been surprised to see an admirable complete set of Jekyll titles in facsimile emerging at very reasonable prices before the magic deadline. There is no skull duggery. Quite the contrary. The Antique Collectors Club, who are publishing them, simply had the original idea of actually paying the copyright holders, Miss Jekyll's estate, rather than waiting in order not to have to.

The Antique Collectors Club is an enterprising little company at Woodbridge in Suffolk, run by John Steel and his wife Diana, who manages the printing side of the business on the same premises. They have made a good job of reproducing the Jekyll texts and the black-and-white photographs of such books as *Garden Ornaments*. They are even reproducing George Elgood's marvellous watercolours for *Some English Gardens*.

Rather than provide an exegesis to each or all the volumes, John Steel recommends the recently published study of Jekyll and her architect partner Edwin Lutyens in Jane Brown's *Gardens of a Golden Afternoon*. You could not do better for an understanding of what the partners did, where, how and for whom. It is a first-rate piece of both scholarship and plantsmanship in its own right. It also goes a long way towards explaining why Gertrude Jekyll's gardens are almost all in the past tense. Within a year of her death, it is said, Miss Jekyll's own garden was virtually unrecognizable. Her creations were so incredibly labour- and knowledge-intensive that they could not last.

—December—

AGRONYM?

Why couldn't the NCCPG have thought of some pithier set of initials? Unless the whole title is spelt out each time, we get ribald letters asking whether we mean the National Collection of Concrete Posts and Gnomes or the ditto of Corpulent Private Gardeners, something to do with the Chelsea Physic Garden (a reasonable thought) or – barbed shaft – the National Council for the Correction of Proofs of *The Garden*. I am told the International Registration Authority has even worse problems.

The National Council for the Conservation of Plants and Gardens is growing apace. Members are expected to do all such good things as may propagate the gospel of conservation (N.S.P.G.C?).

1983

—*January*—

HAPPY NEW YEAR

The month of January makes every diarist cast a look back over the past year, and risk a glance forward to the future, at the way the *oeuvre* is progressing.

I'm sure Jennifer never has this problem in her column. 1 January is: 'Usual six-thirty call; wrote letters; tried a charming new hairdresser in Albemarle Street...' before getting down to the serious business of the day. But then Jennifer is unique, and her subject, fashionable people, is the most unchanging of all.

Working and writing in a garden emphasizes the rolling of the seasons and the sliding of time. It also seems to draw together extraordinary extremes of society and divergences of view. I sometimes reflect here on notable reactions in this column. But they are only a fraction of the underlying feeling that the gardening world, knowledgeable and patient, is waiting out there to comment or quibble on everything we publish.

Months later we are still fielding the reactions from gardeners, boffins, countesses and clerks.

—*February*—

WHO DUNNIT?

Does it not strike you as sinister that a fell disease should have struck one of the flowering cherries last year – and that it just happened to be Kanzan, the purple-pink double that the garden critics love to hate? If Alan Mitchell had been sticking pins into a wax tree I would have expected him to choose the purple plum first...but it is Kanzan that is turning up its toes.

The Forestry Commission reports that many well-established specimens all of this one variety suddenly wilted in June, their leaves turned brown, their twigs and branches died rapidly back, and within a few weeks they were mournful relics – in many cases right down to the graft. Presumably from their lively wild-cherry roots innumerable suckers will arise.

The situation is not at all funny for anyone with a small garden largely given over (as many are) to this vigorous tree. The cause, says the Forestry Commission, is probably a form of canker which also attacks apples, pears, lilacs and magnolias. Weather conditions in 1982 were ideal for its development – and also that of fireblight in apples and pears. Since a similar weather pattern again this year (or for several years) is highly improbable, it may well be that the danger is past. It will be worth watching Kanzan trees with care this summer.

Personally I have a fondness for the plant, lurid as it can be. Like other plants which make strident statements it can easily be misplaced. It looks best in mixed company with plenty of other trees – on the edge of a wood rather than solo in a suburban garden.

—March—

NETHER REGIONS

I managed to fit my first-ever visit to New Zealand into the middle of a working trip to Australia in December. However different you expect the two countries to be the reality still comes as a shock…and in nothing more than their plants. The Tasman Sea, less than a three-hour flight away, separates two warm-temperate worlds of plants that might almost be on two planets.

It was not high season in December for the native flowers of either country – especially with eastern Australia toasted like a biscuit by an interminable drought. Town and suburban gardens were full of exotic northern-hemisphere plants blooming unperturbed. One of the stranger sensations was walking under a glorious green avenue of healthy elms in a Melbourne park and to note how each tree had a watering trough gouged in the grass beside it which a gardener filled every morning.

I have always thought of the pastures of Victoria as evoking (with their clumped and dotted gum trees) nothing so much as the ghost of an English park, its greens turned to browns and ashen grey. The land-scape round Auckland, in total contrast, is almost Devonian with its tangled green hedges and well-watered grazing. Kiwi-fruit orchards are conspicuous for their geometrical windbreaks of poplars; an agreeably formal touch. (Actinidias and their fashionable fruit suffer badly from wind damage.) Alas, the native Kauri, Rimu and southern beech are little in evidence – the forest plantations are uniformly the dark, dull but vigorous Monterey pine.

Tasmania was the high point of this trip. The little island supplies the missing link between the Australian and New Zealand floras: the only place where eucalyptus and southern beech are both natives. The scale and beauty of the unspoilt Tasmanian 'bush' astonished me. An hour from the busy northern town of Launceston a friend has planted a flourishing vineyard within sight of the sea in a land-scape of quite moving purity: towering stands of white gums, thick-ened with blackwood (the deep green wattle *Acacia melanoxylon*), alternating with rich pasture in a way that would have sent Repton into rhapsodies.

We flew over the mountains to the west coast to see the Gordon and Franklin rivers, whose projected damming for hydroelectric power is causing such controversy. It seems scarcely possible that in a world where everyone pays lip-service to conservation local politics can still threaten such a sublime piece of wilderness.

The rivers foam down from the 4,000-foot central plateau through a temperate jungle of rare tree species, notably the Huon pine, *Dacrydium franklinii*, cutting gorges accessible only by raft or several days of trekking. It is the world in its fragile innocence: the antipodes that Cook and Banks marvelled at.

If government has its way the innocence has not long to live. The dam will drown the gorges; roads and power lines will scar the moun-tains. As witness to the power of pollution a whole peak downwind of the copper mine at Queenstown is already bare rock.

Permanent jobs for almost 30 people, I was told, are to be created by sacrificing this great virgin wilderness.

—May—

OUTLOOK CHANGEABLE

I sometimes ponder on the contrast between the idea that gardening is a well-planned and orderly drill and the chaotic reality. You know the often-painted picture of the winter evenings with seed catalogues, the plotting of crops in rotation, the notebooks full of last summer's jottings crystallizing in new planting plans, the nicely judged pruning and the deep, even mulch.

Ah well, I tell myself, I'm sure Wisley is like that. All you need is the training, and of course the time. It's these quick dashes out between articles and chapters that always seem to be frustrated by gales or frost or drenching rain. Should writers not garden? Certainly an awful lot of gardeners write, but for them I suppose the quick dash is to the typewriter between pricking out and potting something on.

It was early February that brought on these frustrated thoughts. January was roaring gales: the noise in the potting shed under the poplars was like the fo'c'sle of a barque rounding the Horn. Then came those gentle days of deceptive warmth and calm when buds swelled as you watch; crocuses flung back their petals and even daffodils came under starter's orders. The list of jobs on my desk grew longer and more urgent. Productivity plummeted. Scarcely had I reached the door when brilliant sunshine turned to gloom and the first snowflakes fell. Boots off; back to the desk – and the sky had cleared.

Day after day we played at cat and mouse, we amateurs and the sky. Cold fronts came rolling steadily out of the west like missile launchers on May Day. Then just as suddenly the parade stopped. Snow covered the bulbs and froze on the swelling buds. Its cold brilliance whitewashes the ceilings still. The roses have just arrived, and been added to the list of urgent jobs...

—July—

PURE GOLD

I am afraid the RSPCGF may pounce on me when they read this, but I must recount the extraordinary biography of my goldfish. Two years ago when we built our conservatory I installed an old lead cistern, fixed to the wall and plumbed with a miniature circulating pump and spout to provide a pretty splashing sound. I decided to experiment with goldfish, bought three tiddlers and popped them in. I fed them conscientiously for a while, but sad to say two floated up lifeless. Of the third I could find no trace.

Over a year later when I was cleaning the water I discovered to my delight that number three was still present and correct, flitting shyly through the depths, exactly the same tiny size as when I installed him, having survived on nothing whatsoever but the nourishing effluents of a lead tank. He is still with us, does not seem interested in the food I now offer him, but shows no sign of undernourishment (except undersize). Should I give him a new companion, have him tested for brain damage, or just leave him alone? And what should we call him? Leadbelly was one suggestion. Someone else said Plumb.

CYPRIOT SPRING

Friends have been urging me for years to visit Cyprus in the spring to see the flowers. They were right. We spent a short holiday near Paphos in late March and found ourselves in Arcadia, with flower-filled meadows stretching innocently from the Troodos mountains to the brink of the wine-dark sea.

The Greek inhabitants are inevitably developing parts of the coast that conservationists would rather see untouched, but the land and seascape along the west coast of the island, and particularly around the ancient village of Polis to the north, is moving in its ancient unspoilt beauty and innocence.

Best of all, to me, was a day spent driving up into the Troodos mountains to see the unique forest of Cyprus cedars, *Cedrus brevifolia*, that entirely fills a narrow valley high up among the otherwise pine-covered slopes. The needles of Cyprus cedars are about half the length of those of the familiar cedar of Lebanon, so its similarly tabular formations in maturity are even more exaggerated by its short-cropped air. Oddly, about half the trees were healthily blue-green, the other half yellowish and chlorotic looking; half tall and straight as masts, the other half stunted into Quasimodo attitudes. To add to the pleasure, the bottom of the valley along the stream was lined with enormous specimens of the oriental plane, with their creamy bark. They never make straight trunks, but writhe like pale and bulky serpents among the dark ramrods of the cedars.

—*August*—

THE JUNGLE IN THE CITY

Those who have found it hard to love the draughty sterility of the Barbican may change their minds when they see the Conservatory, which all this summer has been a hive of gardeners busy in a sort of technicolor jungle of rampaging sub-tropical plants, although at present it is not certain when their efforts will be open to the public.

Whatever reservations I have about the building, there will soon, it seems, be very little of it visible as the vines scramble to the rafters and creep along the overhanging terraces. One magnificent species, the Indonesian 'chestnut vine', *Tetrastigma voinierianum*, is already threatening total takeover with its fleshy tendrils. A multitude of bougainvilleas, acacias, orchids, tropical figs, araucarias and other less-familiar exotics fills the strange greenhouse four stories high, with three galleries contributing their cargo of plant life to the heady display. Wisley has contributed complete duplicates of its collections of coleus and fuchsias to enrich an already amazing palette of colour. Coming soon, I am told, are hot-house butterflies, too, in case the colour be accused of standing still.

PERSEVERANCE PAYS

The saga of the Giardino Botanico Hanbury at La Mortola, the long-drawn-out rescue attempt of the loveliest of botanic gardens from the clutches of Italian bureaucracy, has drawn many a cry of 'Wolf' – and I am one of those who has raised false hopes in the past.

But today, this sixteenth day of May in the year of our Lord one thousand nine hundred and eighty three, the wolf has finally appeared on cue. Lupo Osti, a true son of Romulus and the most dogged of the Italian partisans in this international cause, reports from Rome that all the parties concerned in the transfer of the gardens from the Ministry of 'Beni Culturali' to the University of Genoa have now signed documents signifying their agreement. The Rector of the University has reconvened his Advisory Committee. There seems a fair prospect of the great garden, on its peerless promontory where Italy meets France, being restored to at least a shadow of its former glories.

—October—

OVERSEASONED

Since the elms died, the sight of the merest brown leaf in the crown of a healthy tree of any kind has been enough to startle me. What holocaust is coming next? The sight of sadly disfigured, and some dead, plane trees in Trafalgar Square this summer gave me a terrible fright. Are we to see the planes dying too?

John Gibbs, chief pathologist at the Forestry Commission, has an explanation which is reassuring, but also a warning. He blames the ill health, particularly of youngish street-side trees, largely on the lavish use of salt on the roads in the '81-'82 winter. Exactly how the salt reaches the roots (through the roadway? through the drains?) is not clear. But the roots ingest it: the chloride levels in the leaves a year later proves the fact.

In addition, the very wet spring this year was ideal for the development of anthracnose, a fungus that kills young growth. Planes normally recover with new shoots in summer, but trees weakened by salt can fail to do this.

Happily the biggest old planes in parks and squares are relatively safe and seem in their massive stability to resist bad attacks of anthracnose. But Trafalgar Square and other roadside sites can ill afford to lose their planes. Could we try a lighter hand with the salt?

—November—

LAMMAS BONUS

It has been a momentous year for growth on young trees and shrubs. The deluge of spring and the warm summer have combined to add almost incredible shoots to many of the juveniles whose progress I watch with neurotic concentration.

The second spurt of oaks putting on summer wood has been particularly spectacular: one Caucasian oak, *Quercus macranthera*, only 7-feet high last year, put on a healthy 18 inches in spring, then in July suddenly leapt up nearly another yard. When I pinched out the tips of some side branches to encourage the leading shoot, the tree responded with a gesture very like putting its tongue out: the last leaves on the pinched–out tips just went on growing into great cabbage-sized excrescenses, one of them 14 x 6 inches.

This spring the English oaks in particular suffered even more than usual from a spring aphis attack. Their foliage was covered with sticky secretion, rapidly turned near-black, and must have been photosynthesizing with one arm tied behind its back.

The brilliant pink and pale green of the Lammas shoots, contrasting vividly with the black older leaves, was a beautiful sight. It made me wonder whether this is perhaps one of the reasons for a second batch of shoots in mid-summer: to have clean efficient leaves to carry on photosynthesis when the old ones are clogged up.

MONOPLANTING

It is not often that you see a garden that achieves the desirable quality of unity by the direct method: having only one kind of plant. Rose gardens are the one common exception; but the variety of colours almost always weakens the effect.

I often fantasize about making an enclosure within the garden which will be an uncompromising monoculture. Why? Because I suspect that if it worked it would give visitors a more memorable picture to carry away with them than almost anything I am likely to achieve in the way of subtle painting with colours, or grouping of forms. Perhaps I am saying that most of us need a good sock in the eye to make us start paying attention.

There are more plants than one might think that would form a picture and create an atmosphere worth imbibing at any season. One of the most striking enclosures I can remember is a sort of camellia orchard, closely hedged in with bamboos, in Dr Jimmy Smart's garden at Marwood Hill near Barnstaple.

Not a single one of the camellias was in flower when I was there – but no matter. The deep lustre and glitter of their leaves, cut off from the world by the tall bamboos, was enough. It has lodged in my mind and given me pleasure many times since.

Bamboos form another picture I shall never forget, too: just a beautifully groomed rod, pole or perch of them, well-mulched and well-separated by removing old canes, against a white stucco wall in a Kyoto monastery.

One of my current fantasies is a phalanx of fatsias. Perhaps two short walks crossing at right angles between four solid blocks of dark, glistening, enormous fingered leaves of claret-bottle green, lightened in autumn with globes of pale green ivy flowers. To heighten the jungle effect I might plant a palisade of *Ailanthus*, the tree of heaven, or the even bigger-leaved *Cedrela sinensis* to hem it in and roof it over. Or use a lovely Japanese willow, *Kinuyanagi*, that I spotted in the new arboretum at Wisley, its silky leaves in clusters at the branch tips, looking almost like a featherweight palm tree. (I will probably never do it, but its more fun than counting sheep.)

Aren't we, seriously, though, too easily lured by variety? Single-mindedness is particularly appropriate in public places, where standard mixtures of plants frequently fail to produce any effect whatsoever. There are few opportunities for planting avenues nowadays. I am suggesting bringing the confident spirit of the avenue into confined spaces, to print bold images of plants onto minds that find focusing difficult in a jumble of shapes and colours.

— *December* —

The Desert Blooms

I could hardly believe my eyes this August when Betsy Barlow, the remarkable young Administrator of New York's Central Park, took me to see the latest transformation. We went right up town on the east side, where the park abuts on one of the toughest areas in the city. There, a stone's throw from the busy street, is a large and lovely formal garden of perennials, round a fountain planted with a distinctly English eye for soft harmony and quiet beauty. There was not a guard in sight, no graffiti; just the neighbourhood appreciating what must be its most beautiful corner by far.

The Administrator's secret seems to be quiet determination to clean up, restore and offer Olmsted's masterpiece back to New York. Not only the dedicated supervizors and their gangs of volunteers but the reaction of the public show that human nature is too often underrated.

1984

— April —

VARIEGATIONS ON A THEME

How wonderfully clubbable gardeners are. I thought there were already specialist fan clubs for every conceivable group of plants. But now I hear from Michael Warren (whose splendid photographs so often appear on the pages of *The Garden*) that he and a group of sympathizers who get a thrill from a lack of chlorophyll are starting a Variegated Plant Contact Group. Lovers of the blotched or painted leaf from Nottingham and Norfolk to Devon have already made contact, and a register of plants that occur in variegated forms is being drawn up.

I once saw a nineteenth-century Japanese book on variegated plants in four fat volumes, all illustrated with black-and-white drawings. It made me wonder how many plants there are which have not, sometime, somewhere, sported a variegated leaf. But unless a practised propagator happens to be at hand, nature rapidly withdraws her offer.

— May —

METEOROLOGIC

If Chelsea were held in the first week of June the chances would be four-to-one in favour of dry weather. It may be statistical nonsense, but it is great fun going back over one's weather records to see what happened when.

The odds above are based on the weather in Essex over the past five years. There has only been one wet first week in June. On the other hand there have been three out of five wet third weeks in May – the week of Chelsea. In fact May is one of the wettest months, with a five-year average (here) of about 4.5 inches out of an annual 20. The wettest May of the five was last year, when oddly enough the third week was the one dry spell.

On the whole wet Mays are followed by dry Junes and the one very dry May (1980) by a wet June – though not the first week. What is my prediction for Chelsea this year? In our departing President's immortal words: 'the best Chelsea ever'.

FIGHTING TALK

'Plant material is one of the supremely vulgar phrases of our language and I hope if anybody has been using it he will stop immediately. Plants are not materials. The phrase is commonly used by people of careless habits, indifferent brains and, I suspect, no morals whatever'.

Not William Robinson, but Henry Mitchell, the gardening correspondent of the Washington Post. For those who can take their gardening journalism robust, Mitchell is a find. 'Nothing in all gardening requires so much work for so little return as a rock garden' is another of his *obiter dicta*.

AN EYE FOR AN EYE

The Tate Gallery is having a retrospective exhibition of the work of a painter who was at the same time a great gardener, Welshman and East Anglian: Cedric Morris. At his house in Suffolk, Benton End near Hadleigh, he ran – or perhaps 'held' is a better word – a painting school of an informal kind for 40 years, encouraging scores of amateur painters to express themselves as freely with their brushes as their uninhibited master.

The spirit of Benton End survives on canvas. But Morris's eye for plants has another memorial in the work of Beth Chatto, who knew him for 30 years. Many of her 'unusual' plants, the bold hellebores and graceful alliums that she has shown with such flair and with so wide an influence, came from Cedric Morris's garden. The show at the Tate is the formal memorial, but the torch has been passed on.

— *August* —

FEMININE FLATTERY?

The most handsome compliment that a desirable plant can pay its gardener is to produce a crop of seedlings. A single seedling from a favourite specimen is perhaps the most exciting find of all. Why, you ask yourself, did just one seed germinate and flourish? Why just there? Would it have obliged if I had sown it myself? Teasing imponderables, these, that make weeding a constant adventure. Among the ground-sel, the ivy, the chickweed and nettles and worse, suddenly there is a beautiful little hellebore, an oaklet, a rose with intriguing leaves...or even an apparently total stranger.

'Miss Willmott's Ghost' must have turned up as a mystery, if the legend be true that she scattered its seed in gardens that she liked. Anyone who has been baffled by a vividly white-variegated version of honesty, with pure white flowers, springing up in a garden where I have been wandering, may regard it as Tradescant's Ghost. Don't exorcize it. It is one of the brightest plants of May.

If an unexpected seedling is a treat, even more so can be an unlooked-for sport; a branch that suddenly has a new idea – not to be confused with reversion, which slips back into an old habit.

I gave a friend some cuttings of the Paris daisy, the fine grey-leaved, single-white-flowered *Chrysanthemum frutescens*. It came to me from the Aga Khan's gardens in Sardinia. A particularly pale and pretty form, I thought.

This year one of her plants has apparently decided that white is old hat. Also that a single row of petals is hardly worth bothering with. A lusty branch with double pink flowers is taking over. I have begun to watch my own plants with interest – and a touch of suspicion. Is there a feminist underground at work?

...AND ITS SINCEREST FORM

I freely admit that when I take my Yellow Book in hand on a summer afternoon and go shopping round other people's gardens, one of my main motives is to plagiarise. As Tom Lehrer put it: 'Let no-one else's work evade your eyes...but remember to call it research.'

This is the season for seeing how well (or badly) plants work together; what creates a muddle and what a subtle blend; what a bold effect and what a strident mess; what plants retire early in the summer and call for reinforcements of colour and interest.

If I had to pick out a single piece of memorable planting from this season's visiting it would be a billowing mass of *Euphorbia wulfenii*, the king of spurges, like a wave breaking against a wall, and here and there throwing up spurts of brilliant blue – the plumes of equally regal echiums. Admittedly the wall was in northern California; the front of the Chappellets' long low ranch high above the Napa valley. Molly Chappellet is one of those gardeners who uses the majestic scale of her rugged surroundings – peaks, valleys and lakes you can see for 50 miles – to make her garden feel like an intimate room within, and not intimidated by, the landscape. Big plants in strong groups are a show of confidence. They buttress intricate planting and subtle harmonies of colour that would be pygmied by the sweep of hills and sky.

Of all the long-lasting minor ornaments of the latter summer, to reinforce (and bemedal) a shrub that has retired on its pension for the year, I would choose *Tropaeolum speciosum*, the miniature scarlet trophy-faced climber that scrambles, where it is happy, up bushes and trees, and even weaves through lawns. The books say it likes acid soil and rain. Happily my Essex plants are illiterate, and clamber eagerly from alkaline dust up into yews and cypresses.

—*September*—

WHOSE FAULT?

I've often thought that the Wisley coroner has a pretty doleful job. Day after day parcels of small cadavers, or a limb or a leaf to save postage, turn up in dozens with plaintive notes from the bereaved. 'It looked so healthy when I planted it. I watered and fed it faithfully. The first little leaves looked so vigorous. And then they withered. I watered it frantically. A little sprout appeared at the bottom. But it died. It seemed to have no will to live.'

The post-mortem report I seem to get most often is headed Faulty Root Action. For some reason or other, it tells me, the roots didn't do their stuff properly. Roots matter. No roots, no plant. But why didn't they? Who was the one at fault? They may have come from the nursery curling round in the pot like Corrievrechan but I teased them out and spreadeagled them properly in a sumptuous mixture of peat and compost, sand, sieved soil, bonemeal...I didn't stint.

One or two little trees, this spring, lost their first leaves to frost. Why they didn't have the vim to have a second go I don't know. Most often I suspect drought – and certainly there was no rain from the end of January until mid-May. But the ground was moist, and I watered like a monsoon. Did I drown them? This (too late) was my alternative theory. The root action was faulty because there was not enough drainage. My fault.

I haven't dug them up yet. I won't until they have withered or rotted to the point where a new shoot seems impossible. But even at this stage I have been proved wonderfully wrong. A few years ago I cut down a dead redwood that the nursery had delivered with too much top and too little root. The next year a sprightly young shoot was pushing through the grass from beside the apparently lifeless stump. Be impulsive anywhere except in the garden.

— October —

CONSERVATORY NOTE

It is quite a while since a conservator's note appeared in this diary. For once I am speaking not of conservation but the conservatory. Faithful readers may remember that this particular delight of Trad's is now four years old, a lapse of time in which optimistic ignorance should have succeeded to a degree of experience.

This is a potty conservatory: only pots; no beds. The theory is that we can thus have the best of all seasons by juggling pots between conservatory and greenhouse. A more methodical operator would by now have mastered the art and have a rich palette every week of the year. The reality is not so rosy: if you want big plants, climbers really covering walls, you must have big pots. And big pots need something like a fork-lift truck to move them.

All the same it is hard not to be happy with the summer jumble of geraniums and fuchsias, white oleander, airy bamboo, and pale blue plumbago starred with dark red passion flowers. Blue gum and lemon-scented gum threaten to burst through the roof. The graceful strawberry vine embraces the leaden tropical leaves of *Tetrastigma voinerianum*. My biggest pot can't be big enough for this giant climber. It has sulked all season. Probably it needs feeding with dead crocodiles. A generous visitor last year gave us a little tree from New Zealand, *Leucaena leucocephala*, with ferny fronds and pale yellow paintbrush flowers. Grevilleas, acacias, oranges and lemons, an olive and a 'heavenly bamboo', Japan's noble *Nandina*, cluster in a wild jumble of nationalities and complexions, shading an understorey of ferns.

A conservatory needs a lot of valeting to look really spruce. Daily deadheading, as well as daily watering. I can't say Trad's always gets it, because reading the paper and drinking tea are very time-consuming operations. And there is nowhere more pleasant to perform them than at the little round table among the pots.

RESPECT FOR OUR ELDERS

The elder is too ready a volunteer in most gardens to be regarded as much better than a weed. But nibbling a delicious creamy elderflower sorbet last June, reflecting on its subtle summery hint of muscat, it struck me that it is one of the great, if somewhat eccentric, characters of our countryside.

What other plant provides us with such abundance of fragrant and edible flowers as well as fruit? To the wine-lover the flowers offer poor man's Moselle; the fruit poor man's port. Over a century ago in fact laws had to be passed in Portugal to prohibit the use of elderberries to improve real port in colour and sugar content. It is an odd fact, for which I know no explanation, that to this day orchards of elder trees are found up back roads in the port country.

Still more curious is the contrast between the scents, delicate and rich, of the plant's organs of generation, and the stink of its leaves and wood. Elder boughs keep the flies off mules' faces. I have to wash my hands after pruning an elder tree.

Consider, though, some of its wayward sports. I noticed more than one exhibitor at Chelsea this year using small plants of its copper-coloured form for its foliage. The plant is even more charming when its flower heads turn out to be pink. The relatively common variegated form, 'Marginata', is one of the brightest, and certainly one of the most vigorous, of cream-splashed shrubs. 'Aurea', the golden elder, can be a pleasant warm yellow. *Bean* speaks of weeping, fastigiate and round-leaved forms which I have not seen.

My own favourite is 'parsley-leaved' elder – 'cut-leaved' would be a more accurate description. 'Laciniata' is the official name. It combines the domestic virtues of its tribe with a texture, grey-green, quiet and intricate, found in no other plant that I know.

—November—

RIVIERA RENAISSANCE?

There is positive news of progress at La Mortola that will please anyone in whom hope still triumphs, however precariously, over scepticism. This most precious Riviera garden, the creation of the Hanbury family over generations, has been at the mercy of Italian bureaucracy for more than a decade.

This month a new figure steps on to the scene, carrying all our hopes with him. He is Dr Michael Lear, the horticultural botanist who has established an international reputation for his cataloguing work for the National Trust and the Royal Botanic Gardens at Kew. He has accepted a two-year visiting professorship at Genoa University, the new guardian of the garden. His presence at La Mortola, and his eventual methodical survey of the rarities the gardens contain, will be crucial to the reinstatement of the garden to its former glory.

O TEMPORA, O FLORES

It was a long time since I had been to Versailles, and revelled in the superlative statuary, the grandeur of the *Orangerie* and its palms, the mossy fountains in the woods, and the vistas seemingly without end. I had forgotten how amidst all the formality of the relentless *allées* there are wide spaces (particularly around the Trianon) where well-spaced trees have matured to magnificent specimens in enough pasture to give an almost English feeling. All this is in superb condition.

I was specially curious, though, after a note from a Member, Professor Faegri, castigating the choice of bedding in the parterres. Having praised the parterres of the Jardin de Luxembourg I had expected something equally apt at Versailles. I can only say that Professor Faegri is absolutely right. The plants are not only historically inappropriate but luridly tasteless. What's more, they are the same wherever you go. The lovely walk to, and through, the Grand Trianon ends in complete anti-climax with the same beastly bedding.

If historical accuracy is to be ignored why not make that beautiful half-walled garden into a formal roseraie with bowers and swags between pillars? That would be worth wandering in. Perhaps le Nôtre could send a sign of some sort.

1985

— *February* —

LOOK, NO GLOVES

Alan Titchmarsh, always sprightly and stimulating on the radio, has had a go at doing for gardening what the Sloane Ranger books have done for, presumably, ranging. Under the title *The Avant-Gardener*, Titchmarsh touches on all the soft spots of those who have to 'get things right' – even in gardening. 'What to Wear', for example. 'Nowhere in the garden is the Royal influence more noticeable than in clothing.' Happily there are drawings of a vaguely Royal-looking Him and Her leaning on their spade and hoe respectively. My memory needed a jog: it seems ages since I saw a Royal hoeing – let alone noticed what She was wearing.

But I don't know whether to be proud or ashamed of my unfashionable gardening gear. I have got it all wrong, from my black Wellies (they should be green 'Hunters', with straps unbuckled) to the headgear. Did you know (I didn't) that He should never wear gloves? Its impossible to hide my huge leather gauntlets (made, I fancy, for protection from a furnace, but sovereign against roses and even brambles).

In every other department I'm in the same sort of trouble. If I admit that I enjoy azaleas in pots indoors, use lawns and possess not a single maze, nor even a knot, grow carrots and brussels sprouts, and to cap it all have just cut down a *Metasequoia* for firewood, the Avant-Gardener will know just how far beyond the pale I am.

— *March* —

THE DARTFORD WONDER

I cannot tell you whether when you read this the prodigy will still be there. *The Guinness Book of Records* has recorded the facts, but the denouement is up in the air.

In April 1979, Mr Les Stringer, a sheet metal-worker with green fingers, planted a cutting of a 'Black Hamburgh' vine against the wall of his works canteen by the River Darenth at Dartford in Kent. That year it produced two bunches of grapes. In 1980, building up strength, it produced 139 bunches. In 1981 its 2,007 bunches weighed 274 pounds; in 1982, 4,000 bunches weighed nearly three times as much; in 1983, 7,620 bunches weighed over 1,000 pounds, and last year 6,780 bunches weighed nearly 1,500 pounds.

The Dartford Wonder Vine, now nearly six years old, has a stem circumference of over one foot and spreads about 130 feet along the factory wall. No other 'great vine' on record appears to have grown so prodigiously or cropped so immoderately. It is a wonder that any of the Darenth survives to meet the Thames after the vine has had a drink.

But the vine has its problems. The water authorities are tidying up the riverbank and the vine is in the way. Mr Stringer has asked me to help. At this stage I can only say I am trying. Wouldn't you?

SHRUB OF GOOD CHEER

We were discussing our first choice in small shrubs the other day when I looked out of the window (it was drizzling darkly) and spotted what is surely one of the great all-rounders for limited space: the cheerful-looking perfumed *Daphne odora* 'Aureo-marginata'.

Many daphnes are temperamental, or short-lived, or both. I daren't mention one or two in this garden in case they should get wind of it and resign forthwith. Touch wood, *C. o.* 'A-m' keeps spreading slowly, not more than three feet high but potentially much wider. I grow it in a fairly sheltered wall-border, facing southish. When its rosy pointed buds open to apple-blossom pink their scent can reach across a courtyard. I love the mezereon, too (especially the white one), not to mention the showy 'Somerset', the formal, dark little *D. retusa* – or even to whisper the names of *D. b* or *D. g*. But for all round good humour I think I know the winner – and I urge you to plant one, too.

– *April* –

BY THEIR BOOKS...

The leading plantsman and the most revered garden-maker of their generation died in the same week in January. Sir Harold Hillier and Russell Page each stood in a class apart: wholly dedicated men whose names are secure in the history of horticulture.

Harold Hillier's greatest achievement was the Hillier nursery catalogue. Even as a literary compilation it was awe-inspiring: so much practical knowledge and lucid judgement so succinctly expressed. But to have made it a commercial reality – you could actually buy, or at any rate order and eventually receive, almost any of some 7,000 kinds – that was the work of a quite exceptional nurseryman, far beyond the call of duty, or even of commercial prudence. We, the beneficiaries of his great achievement, had no right to expect a single nursery to be the conservator of such a range of plants. We were disappointed when, inevitably, it proved impracticable and the nursery list was cut down to realistic proportions. But by then, Sir Harold had given his collection, in the form of Jermyns Arboretum, to the County of Hampshire. His work has not been lost; we will only miss the luxury of ready access to it to enrich our own gardens.

Strangely enough, Russell Page's name will be best remembered, too, for a single book: *The Education of a Gardener*. As a professional landscaper he worked, in the main, in discreetly private gardens, many of them abroad. Few of us have seen, or ever will see, a great deal of his work. But his 'Education' is there for us all to read, and nobody who claims to be in earnest about gardening, or to be interested in more than the mere mechanics of the art, can afford not to study this inspired and inspiring book in depth.

It were impudent to try to expound so thorough a thinker in a note, or even by quoting him. (First prize for impudence – and cant, too – goes to the author of *The Times* obituary, who wrote that Russell Page was most interested in 'the mystery of the space between plants'.) Speaking of garden ornaments, Russell Page wrote, 'The artifacts of a garden should be summary, direct and apposite'. Nobody knew better than he the meaning, and the application, of those three admirable attributes.

ROSES AND RAPTURES

According to *Science Now* our ability to detect smells declines markedly with age. I wonder if experienced gardeners are aware of this. Do the roses and lilies of youth smell stronger, or more distinctly and characteristically, than the same flowers in old age?

In the field of wine-tasting, where sense of smell is all-important, I have never known anyone remark that older tasters are less acute.

Rather the reverse, in fact. But then who can say how far experience counterbalances any decline in nostril power? Certainly the most perceptive writing about the scents of flowers comes from such people as Graham Stuart Thomas and Christopher Lloyd, whose experienced noses have seen enough seasons to have marked, learned and inwardly digested.

— *June* —

ON THE BOX

One evening recently I had the double treat of watching two good gardening programmes on television. Two, mark you, in one evening. First there was a saunter round the delectable Botanic Gardens at Christchurch, New Zealand, extremely well conducted, letting the splendid plants make their own impression: no frenzied hyperboles, just an intelligent and useful commentary. Then there was one of Granada's Wisley programmes, with the staff going sensibly about their business. Again, no high-pressure selling, just a girl in a khaki jumper who loves her houseplants, and knows how to care for them.

You don't need a long memory to recall when nearly all television gardening stuck to one tired formula – and the programmes that didn't should have done. The morning after a demonstration of planting lettuces – I think it was lettuce – my friend Ken Akers (a Cockney, as you'll see) said, 'I wonder where he got that soil. Harrods, I bet'.

I am being a little unfair. There have been such memorable eccentricities as *The Front Garden*, when Candida Lycett-Green drew out wonderful asides from her subjects. (Man clipping colossal topiary pheasant, of neighbour with a rival bird: 'That's just a chicken'.) But not many. Nobody ever sounded so bored to such purpose as Sir John Gielgud doing garden history.

So let us be grateful. The powers behind the box, or some of them, are getting gardening right at last.

—August—

AVE ATQUE VALE

This evening the garden looks as though a ferocious giant has just blundered through it, lashing out at everything in reach of his stick. At three o'clock this afternoon hail such as I have never seen came banging and bouncing out of a suddenly black sky. In a moment the ground was white, and golf balls were cannoning about in all directions, raising great splashes as they hit the brimming gutters so that the house walls were running with water. In the conservatory, where I had dodged the first skirts of the downpour, things quickly became very obviously unsafe. The hammering of ice on glass was so loud that I knew the glass would go. I had lowered the outside cedar-slat roller blinds against the afternoon sun. Ice balls started to split and smash the cedar first, then with triumphant jangling the panes of the roof.

Retreating into the house from the deluge of glass, water and ice, I realized that not only the conservatory but the leaded lights in the house and even the thick clay tiles of the roof were falling like infantry squares to a machine-gun. In 15 minutes it was over: the drive, the yard, the terrace awash with water trapped by ice, mixed in a salad of shredded leaves. Beneath every tree half its canopy of young foliage lying in a circle; the soft growth, the flower heads, the leading shoots of every plant in the garden had been dashed to the ground. In the sudden quiet as the hail stopped, leaving its manna three inches deep, a pearly mist arose to hide the devastation. I wondered how wide the storm had been, thinking of the nurseryman's glass down the road. And I understood more clearly than ever why the owners of vineyards, particularly the smallholder proprietors of Burgundy, like to have their parcels scattered here and there over several villages, despite the inconvenience. To see a year's income put through the shredder must be a chastening experience.

The sad bit about my story is that this year our pair of swans had a brood of three cygnets for the first time. One was killed by a direct hit and a second one wounded: whereupon the parents turned against their remaining young so that we had to rescue them. Two cygnets are now in the loving care of the Kirby family, a veritable Barnardo's for misplaced small creatures. Swans don't stay small for long, though.

— *September* —

THE FROZEN SOUTH

Anyone who has visited the south of France or Italy as far south as Tuscany this summer past has seen dismal evidence of the severity of last winter. Near Florence in May, I could scarcely believe the whole hillsides of dead olive trees. Later in south-west France I drove past kilometres of dead hedges of macrocarpa, and even on the Atlantic coast looked with awe at tall Monterey pines, brown from top to toe.

In Nice I am told the palm trees along the Promenade des Anglais may be dead, leaving the municipality with a dire problem: where to find hundreds of mature palms. It was a bad winter here, in Kent especially, but not one to change the whole character of the place, as the wholesale death of the most popular exotics would do.

— *October* —

EVERY CLOUD...

The eye that delights in the textures of trees has had a feast this summer past. Torrents at Wimbledon are greeted with modified rapture, but that same telly-celebrated cloudburst (it measured just over three inches here) continued to give me pleasure for a month afterwards in the form of unprecedented fresh summer growth on almost every tree, from the expected pale lammas shoots on oaks to a display on maples, *Sorbus*, birches and shrubby willows in particular that I have never seen before.

I have a bank planted with a collection of the more eccentrically designed willows; willows that glow russet and gleam silver, that flash like whitebeams in May or hang their narrow leaves as mournfully as November rain. Their contrasts of colour, texture and form have never been so telling.

Forming a background the stiff blue brushes of young Scots pines were mingled with ruby stars: new leaves in long sprays on the form of Caucasian maple whose summer growth is always this inflammatory colour. This year we were talking revolution.

— November —

POCKET LANDSCAPES

Every year at Chelsea I find myself turning aside from the forty-course dinner of colour and scent in the marquee to the more austere diet offered by the bonsai displays. There is fascination in these ambivalent midgets suggesting immemorial age. Some are almost pocket landscapes; a whole copse of beech or *Zelkova* spinny. Yet they are, in the strictest sense, horticulture. Precision horticulture, you might call them – like the display of alpines in pots.

— December —

SPADE AND FORK

We are not all the same shape or size; we don't all have the same soil to contend with, and yet to look around you at the range of tools on offer you would almost think we gardeners had been cloned – and our gardens too.

A few years ago I tried to interest manufacturers in making the traditional straight clay spade. No luck at all. They all blamed 'popular demand', and the more impudent among them 'ergonomics', for the fact that all spades today have the handle at an angle to the blade, regardless of whether this design suits either the gardener or garden.

This thought was revived by reading a provocative little paper called *By Hand and Foot*, the organ of the Green River Tool Co. of Brattleboro, Vermont. It tells the story of the Double Digger, a digging fork with six tines and two handles, one at each end.

A similar tool, it says, but with three handles, revolutionized the efficiency of French smallholders in the nineteenth century, doubling the amount of ground that three men could prepare in an hour.

A funny-looking thing like that would never sell here.

1986

—*January*—

THE BEST POLICY

Am I, I wonder, the only member of the Honesty Fan Club? Every spring this unpretentious, almost revoltingly cheerful plant gives me great pleasure – and its more *recherché* forms, more pleasure still.

I looked it up, to see what homely myths attach to its innocent name, in that old standby, Geoffrey Grigson's *English Flora*. Odd. His only reference to Honesty at all is as yet another pseudonym (*nom de terre*?) of Old Man's Beard, Virgin's Bower, or What You Will. (The whole thing sounds more like a Shakespearean comedy than a plant.) Honesty, as every schoolboy knows, is *Lunaria annua*, the magenta-violet-flowered biennial with translucent round papery seedpods that last and last. Not every gardener, however, knows that there are at least two variegated-leaved forms (the leaf margins fading to white). The magenta-flowered one is positively lurid, but a white-flowered one lights up a dark corner, or a dull day, with most charming cheerfulness.

There is also a perennial Honesty, whose flowers are pale pastel-lilac and whose seedpods elegantly narrowed at both ends. Graham Thomas enjoys its colour with *Kerria japonica*. I grow it with *Doronicum plantagineum*, alias Leopard's Bane. Surely Grigson must have something for us on this one. But alas no.

—*February*—

WHAT DOES HE KNOW OF ENGLAND...?

There is probably no more sense in saying that all British gardeners should visit Japan than that all Japanese gardeners should visit Britain...And yet I am not so sure. I have just come back from that strange Looking-Glass Land, and I feel inspired, as I did on my one previous visit, with a new zeal, a new sense of order, a new vision of my own garden.

There are many aspects of the Japanese garden that we do well to study, ideas that we can apply in our gardens without selling our birthright, or turning them into absurd Mikado pastiches.

Am I then going to rake my gravel into water swirls, make fences with bamboo and knots of tarry string, upend a rock among the hostas or tonsure my pines until they look like Buddhist monks?

It would be folly to be so literal. By no stretch of the imagination can I attain the standard of spit and polish that is essential for any self-respecting Japanese garden. If a camellia petal is left lying on the moss it is only because it looks right there – and tomorrow, when it begins to brown, it will be tidied away. I, on the other hand, try to find beauty in drifts of brown leaves, until it becomes glaringly obvious that they are out-of-date – not actually last year's but looking thoroughly reproachful and yellowing the lawn.

It is more in the critical eye that orders composition that I will try to apply Japanese lessons. The famous temples of Kyoto contain within them, in their ordering of space, of form and texture, compositions as perfect in their way as – shall we say – Michelangelo's staircase and the lobby to the library at San Lorenzo. The essence of such design is that the viewer's eye is told exactly what to do; all the aesthetic decisions have been taken.

Japan stirs me to be more decisive, less tolerant, less altogether British about gardening. Friendly old plants that please the heart more than the eye should really be given their quietus. But then is gardening about eyes or hearts? That's another question.

—*March*—

THE BOGEY-MAN

Until last summer the fungus that held centre stage in this garden (apart, that is, from such delicacies as the lawyer's wig and the shaggy inkcap) was the coral spot. A blight of the first water was how I would have classified it; infesting almost any woody plant without notice simply by alighting like an insect and getting to work. By the time its cheerful little red fruiting bodies are on display the bark of its lodging is dead, and at least part of the tree or shrub is a goner.

That was before honey fungus turned up. Try to keep any comforting images of Pooh Bear firmly out of your mind when you encounter this pestilence. Lucky the gardener, I hear you say, who has taken so long to realize what a plague honey fungus can be. The funny thing is how it dawdles about in an area which is impossible to specify or predict, as if it were sampling its potential victims by killing a limb or a clump here or there at random. Then comes a moment of decision and a whole plant is stone dead in a few days. Thus, after I had worried about dead branches in a vigorous birch of the pink-barked kind *Betula albosinensis septentrionalis* growing near an old high garden wall, suddenly a splendid rose, 'Maigold', covering the other side of the wall, turned yellow – the leaves, I mean – wilted and was gone. Shortly afterwards a big smoke bush, of the soft browny purple our Mr Barcock calls his 'West Country Form', looked as though the smoke had turned to fire and consumed the leaves.

I can splash about the Bray's Emulsion in the hope of saving the other plants around. Some, the suppliers point out in their cheerfully fatalistic pamphlet, have reputations for resistance; others quite the reverse. What worries me, though, is the near certainty that the footings of the old wall are infected. I don't expect the pink bricks to turn black and crumble, but I do dread recurring sorties of the sinister black threads from their bunker in the bricks into the surrounding soil and its plants. Unless someone has devized a systemic fungicide for walls, by any happy chance?

—*April*—

LEAD TIME

A brisk walk on a sparkling winter day in the park laid out by William Kent at Rousham House near Oxford. What a pity more gardens are not open in winter: it is, after all, almost half of the life of the garden.

Winter brings many of the loveliest effects of subtle colouring and bold or intricate form that the profligacy of summer hides. The beauty of frost and snow, or the warm low-angled light of a winter's afternoon, are seen only by the owner, or tenant, or gardener.

Kent intended the visitor to encounter the unexpected on his circumambulation. ('Pray, sir,' said Mr Milestone in *Headlong Hall*, 'by what name do you distinguish this character, when a person walks round the grounds for the second time?')

Nothing could have been more unexpected nor unwelcome on my walk, than the sight of the lead statues, masterpieces of modelling and movement cast in 1701 by Jan van Nost, defaced by a horrid layer of flat grey paint. My first thought was that vandals had done this thing. My second was a darker suspicion: that the pedantic hand of a 'conservationist' had been at work. Lead statues of this period, they say, were originally given a coat of paint. But so was the Parthenon – and can you imagine anyone defacing the glowing stone of that antiquity with its original gaudy colours?

Taste has moved on. Lead has a beauty of its own. Its paleness moves us more than eloquence. To obliterate its subtle patina with paint – and battleship-grey paint, at that – is a shocking heresy.

—May—

THE OLD VEG PATCH

That wonder of the horticultural world, the château-gardens of Villandry, should be on the itinerary of every curious person travelling south into western France across the Loire via Tours. A new little booklet on the techniques used to keep its seven hectares trim will add considerably to the fascination of a visit.

It is the vegetable parterre covering a whole hectare that stays most firmly in my mind. Whether it really reproduces a Renaissance garden is beside the point: more credit to its modern creators if it is quite simply a work of their imagination.

To any practical gardener the first dazzling impact of the design is immediately followed by a host of questions as to how on earth the six gardeners manage it. The booklet, called *The Villandry Gardens, Techniques and Plants*, will add enormously to the pleasure of an essential garden pilgrimage.

LET US NOW PRAISE...

The name of John Ray is so little known today, either in comparison with his great scientific contemporaries, Newton and Harvey, his successors Linnaeus and Darwin, or indeed any great naturalist since, that when the Braintree District Council announced a programme of events this summer commemorating Ray it was asked why it was making such a fuss about a recent headmaster of Westminster.

Why Braintree? John Ray was born (in 1627), died (in 1705) and spent most of his life in the village of Black Notley nearby, where his father was the blacksmith.

Why the commemoration? 1986 is the tercentenary of the publication of Ray's *Historia Plantarum* (Vol. I). The consensus of naturalists is that this and his many other books together form the greatest contribution ever made by an individual to natural history. *Historia Plantarum* listed, described and classified 20,000 species of plants. At Cambridge in 1660, Ray had published the world's first ever local flora, a description of the plants of Cambridgeshire. He went on to complete pioneering works on birds, fishes, animals, insects, geology, fossils, anatomy...to compile a three-language dictionary for schools, a glossary of English dialect words, and, in his Wisdom of God Manifested in the Works of Creation, to pave the way for Darwin's theory of evolution.

An adequate account of this quiet man's achievement would take a book, not a diary entry. The inscription from Isaac Newton's memorial can equally be applied to Ray: *Genus humanum ingenio superavit*.

The object of Braintree's initiative, unusual and laudable in a country district council, is to set up a scholarship fund in Ray's memory. The John Ray Trust, which will offer bursaries and scholarships in the branches of science first developed by Ray, numbers among its trustees the Master of his old college, Trinity.

—*August*—

THE CHINK OF CHISELS

One swallow does not a summer make – and this year summer had precious little to do with Chelsea anyway – but looking back over what to me was a hugely entertaining Show I have the peculiar sensation of having detected a trend. It cropped up in all sorts of different guises, but what they all seemed to say was 'let's have more fun'. Plants are not in themselves, or very rarely, objects of entertainment, mirth, or even (except by association) romance. It is all too easy to be po-faced about plants – and hence about gardening in general.

What I think I felt happening around us at Chelsea this year was the resurgence of the picturesque, the consciously romantic, the literary and the frankly funny in design and even in planting: an echo, perhaps, of the spirit of the late-eighteenth and early-nineteenth centuries, in itself a reaction against what was seen (by some) as the pompous monotony of landscapes *à la* Brown. For most mortals the strain of keeping a straight face in front of more and more erudite and refined collections of plants and schemes of planting, of holding one's breath at the mention of a Jekyll border, must eventually become too great. I see an analogy in the cult of chef-worship that threatens at times to come between us and our healthy hunger.

What prompted this idea? A number of quite different stands and gardens. Most prominently, perhaps, the ruined temple by Haddonstone which was so situated that it seemed almost like a preface or portal to the Marquee.

It is as well, perhaps, that as a 'sundries' stand it was not eligible for a medal. The judges might have had problems deciding whether the nettles and brambles were well enough grown. Certainly a beautiful great dandelion in pride of place at the top of a broken column was a prize specimen.

The point of the whole exercise was, of course, to overcome the glaring newness that makes modern garden architecture so fundamentally unromantic and unpicturesque. 'Distressing' reproductions is no new idea, but purposefully bashing about a new temple and planting it with weeds was certainly a memorable departure.

The statuary element was much in evidence everywhere, both outside the Marquee and in, where a splendid old plantsman in bronze peered over his specs at a treasure in a pot. Michael Balston's design for a garden to promote a new scent was powerfully architectural (as well as very pretty). His choice of mop-head bays with the trunks trained as spirals was just the sort of expensive frivolity I am talking about. Another designer carried the feeling to almost cartoon lengths with his huge torso of Neptune popping up from a tiny little pond like a whale in a washtub.

If gardening is about the sensitive selection and placing of plants to create beautiful effects, it is hard for anyone to improve on, for example, Notcutt's stand. It was both a packed gallery of choice plants, and a reminder that stray clumps of cowslips in the grass can be more beautiful than even a *Fremontodendron* in full cry. What was so special about Chelsea this year to me was the evidence of more salt to season all the skill.

—November—

TREES TO TRY

Each time I go to Italy or Greece and see towering cypresses marking out the landscape with their inimitable emphasis I wonder why this family of trees is so little understood in Britain. The only members ever to have been widely planted are 'the macrocarpa' and its half-bred progeny, the Leyland.

The blue-grey Arizona cypress is a relatively familiar (and very attractive) tree. But our enthusiasm seems to end there. There is a sense of daring in planting Italian cypress, *Cupressus sempervirens*. Its association with the Mediterranean makes us think it must be tender. In reality, at least in Essex, it proves hardier than the macrocarpa. That's about where our acquaintance with the true cypresses seems to end. The nursery favourites, in green, yellow and blue, are mostly forms of the ferny 'false cypress' of Oregon, the Lawson – known in its native parts, just to confuse matters, as the Port Orford Cedar.

Now we have a nurseryman who has collected all the known hardy cypresses, and our short-sightedness is revealed.

John Horsman's *Plus Trees* list is the most exhaustive catalogue of conifers grown from seed and available for planting ever published, as far as I know. He is terrific on firs and spruces, prodigious on pines, but of cypresses he has the complete set.

So little known are some of the California species that the only place to read a fairly full account of them is in Alan Mitchell's Forestry Commission publication *Conifers in the British Isles* (1972). He is not as enthusiastic about cypresses (or junipers) as he is about some of the faster-growing and eventually far bigger forest giants. But I have started a little trial of some of John Horsman's species, and what I have seen so far is very pleasing. They grow fast when young, are neat and narrow (if sometimes a trifle severe-looking), and never threaten to become colossal. Very much the sort of thing to adorn a smallish garden, in fact.

I particularly like the very cheerful green of *Cupressus abramsiana*, which at three years is six feet high and has ascending branches like a Lombardy popular. *Cupressus stephensonii*, with short straight branches and knobbly greyish-green foliage, has grown even faster. *Cupressus bakeri* is darker, also going well: this one I have seen in the Arnold

Arboretum in Boston, so it must be very hardy indeed. These three came from central, southern and northern California respectively.

Besides cypresses, there are of course some marvellous pines of less-than-giant size, and such joys as the Korean fir that covers itself with sumptuous purple cones almost from the word go.

A Cool Appraising Glance

If I had been more on the ball I could have recorded the precise bicentenary in April this year of a historic bit of garden visiting. Thomas Jefferson, at that time Minister Plenipotentiary of the United States in Paris, spent from 11 March to 26 April 1786 touring England and regarding our gardens with a critical eye. Jefferson is always worth reading for terse and uninhibited opinions: 'Chiswick. Belongs to the Duke of Devonshire. A garden about six acres; the octagonal dome has a very ill effect, both within and without: the garden shows still too much of art. An obelisk of very ill effect; another in the middle of a pond useless.' 'Stowe...The straight approach is very ill. The Corinthian arch has a very useless appearance...'

Others, such as Esher Place, Caversham, the Leasowes, and especially Blenheim, he loved – although the season he chose, one would have thought, could scarcely have helped.

—December—

Off the Charts

I admire people who wear out colour charts in their methodical search for the ideal colour combinations. I know the greatest borders are composed with painstaking attention to the spectrum. Yet the moments when two or three colours in perfect juxtaposition suddenly thrill the eye are not often, at least in my experience, those that anyone could have planned: it is the fading of one flower as another opens, the unanticipated coincidence of a late flower with an early fruit, or the fleeting tint of an autumn leaf beside a still-fresh bloom that makes you catch your breath.

For several weeks this late summer I have been drawn back again and again to a combination which really only happened by chance. I had popped in a cutting of *Hydrangea villosa* in a bed well populated with the leafy willow gentian. I had certainly not anticipated the effect of mingling the rosy purple of the hydrangea with the gentian's almost sapphire blue.

SIR DAVID SCOTT

Sir David Scott, who died in August at the age of 99, was a true connoisseur of plants and a constantly active and practical gardener until very near the end of his life.

The garden (or 'home for plants', as he called it) which he made over many years at Boughton in Northants, and later shared with his second wife, Valerie Finnis, was a mecca for those who understand and love the intimate realities of gardening. It was not a place where you cast an appraising eye over a mass of colour while chatting about something else. Sir David would, as likely as not, be weeding on hands and knees when you arrived, then lead you through a maze of paths to see a flower you had never seen before, which he thought was 'very pretty' – and which he would subsequently show at the RHS and thus introduce to the gardening world.

The qualities of his mind were such that he would remember the details of a passing conversation a year later. Nothing was off-hand with him. He followed a very distinguished career in public life with a consummate demonstration of how private life can also be led to the highest standards – of courtesy, of judgement, and of kindliness.

CHRISTMAS PRESENT

Trad's letter to Father Christmas is usually pinned to his coverlet beside the largest stocking he can find. But thoughts on Christmas presents are not really out of place in a diary, and might be useful for those with gardeners among their kin.

A leather holster for secateurs is a boon. A folding pocket pruning saw is extremely useful and one never has enough real flowerpots.

1987

— *January* —

OUT OF JOINT

Whether or not we are heading for a new Ice Age I leave to those given to contemplating remote eventualities. That we are experiencing an unwelcome shift in the timing of the seasons my neighbours all seem ready to agree.

Spring gets later and later, and autumn seems reluctant to finish its work before the shortest day of the year.

The trend has been so steady over the past ten years that I can scarcely even get a decent argument over the matter any more. Though I am ready to be convinced, on hearing evidence, that it is confined to eastern England.

But it seems to me to go much further. Is it a complete coincidence, for example, that the vintage season in Bordeaux has seen an unprecedented run of late heat waves? There is nothing in the records to match seven good vintages out of nine: the score since 1978. There is not much support for the Ice Age theory here.

The signs and portents are full of inconsistencies. Rainfall here is both higher and more evenly spread than ten years ago. (Or to put it another way, we no longer suffer from drought.) 1986 was certainly cool, with no sustained mid-summer heat. Yet it also saw the longest frost-free season in my short records. There was none, amazingly, from the middle of March to the end of October – seven-and-a-half months. Not that the spring was warm or came early: it just didn't freeze when it usually does on clear nights in April and May.

Most bizarre manifestation of all: the apparent result of these quirky seasons. By mid-October several plants that we look to to brighten December were already starting to bloom. What has made winter jasmine, *Mahonia* 'Charity', *Camellia sasanqua* and *Viburnum farreri* all catch up with the late-flowering of the roses?

I could write a list of 50 plants in bloom now and offer a prize to anyone who could say what month I was talking about. Delphiniums and winter jasmine? It's a funny year. Rather a pretty colour combination, though.

—February—

PALMY DAYS

It is a sad fact of post-Imperial life that most of the great gardens of what we now call 'the third world' are more or less on their uppers. The splendid exception is Singapore. The political leaders of the tiny island republic only two degrees from the Equator have had the vision to ordain that horticulture be given pride of place. Even the airport at Singapore has its own nursery. You collect your baggage among banks of orchids, and drive into town in the shade of lofty avenues, between walls of flowering shrubs.

A fine cockle-warming topic for February, Trad thought, as he stepped from the relative cool of an air-conditioned taxi into a 90-degree November day.

Singapore takes its gardening very seriously indeed. Its hothouse climate makes planting easy; even the replanting of big trees. But growth is so fast and furious that one of the commonest lorry loads in the city's busy traffic is slashed vines and pruned branches. You feel the surrounding jungle is ready to reclaim the land at the drop of a machete.

All the more remarkable, then, are the Botanical Gardens. Kew itself is scarcely more shipshape. While other tropical botanical gardens are often noble examples of last-ditch devotion by their staff, Singapore, thanks to its political masters, is as *soigné* as it is exciting. One hundred gardeners, in addition to the 20 professional staff, succeed in creating an illusion of romantic serenity in the English style. What difference if it is a python, instead of a fox, that terrorizes the ducks around the very English-looking lake?

The familiar plant names, to a non-tropical plantsman bewildered by the exotica, are mainly those of economic plants, from the sago palm that Marco Polo recorded in Sumatra in 1298 to the rubber trees, *Hevea brasiliensis*, that arrived here as seedlings via Kew in 1877 and still grow where they were first introduced, the foundation stone of the rubber industry in south-east Asia.

One of the tallest trees, 150 feet high and wearing a lightning conductor, is the source of kapok (in the manner of poplar cotton) from its boat-shaped fruits. Another, equally tall, *Erminalia subspathulata*, might almost have been a particularly glorious ash, its spreading top is so feathery and so far from the ground. *Tectona grandis*, the teak tree, looks a trifle like a magnolia.

The palm trees are the sharpest reminder that you are far from home. A perfect avenue of young Royal palms line the road to the herbarium with their elephant-grey trunks. The Malaysian sealing-wax palm, *Cyrtostachys lakka*, has glowing sealing-wax (or lacquer) red leaf stems clasping the upper trunk. And the bamboos, above all the golden bamboos in high-arching clumps on the slopes to the lake, are marvellously familiar and exotic at the same time.

Eleven acres of the garden are true primary jungle, preserved in the heart of the city in all its tangled grandeur (but with a boy sweeping a path through the middle). A substantial extension to the 100 original acres has recently been planted as an arboretum. Along a path of weird cannonball trees from Guinea, with fleshy orange flowers erupting from their spiny trunks, the orchid garden offers a respite with its graceful sprays in gentle colours.

Impressive as this all is, it is made more so by the evidence of scientific organization. All plants are labelled and numbered in a system that divides the whole garden into 'lawns', and an Apple (what else?) computer is being used to try out a new cataloguing system developed by Melbourne University.

Any keen gardener visiting Australia or New Zealand should break the journey to visit this unique and lovely place. Its hotels are splendid – and very welcoming. They have more rooms than guests.

—*March*—

BAMBOOZELUM

I had never heard this marvellous word until I fell in with the fraternity of fanciers of the graceful bamboo who go by the name of the Bamboo Network. Apparently Victorian gardeners, having completed their rockeries, shrubberies and stumperies, went the whole hog planting every bamboo they could find, too.

I imagine the jabberwock term for such a collection arose when the labels went astray, as labels do. Without a confident botanist (and they tend to scatter when bamboos come up) to identify their plants they may well have been bamboozled by their thickets of woody grasses.

For that is what bamboos are. Few modern gardeners (or nurseries) know much about them, and fewer are masters of the magically graceful effects they can produce when they are well sited and well grown – as they are, for example, in Japan.

The object of the Bamboo Network is simply to disseminate information about these neglected plants by putting interested gardeners in touch with each other, and with the few nurseries that grow them.

There is no membership fee. The network is not a society (although I would not be surprised if public interest pushed it in that direction). As its principal mover, Michael Hirsh, says, 'You join by doing, not paying'.

—April—

A QUESTION OF BALANCE

My picture of the perfect garden pond, and I expect yours too, is of placid, translucent water in which brilliant fish can be seen manoeuvering in the depths, as well as flickering about almost within reach.

Water-lilies erupt from their glistening leaves over perhaps a quarter of the surface. On the margin water-hyacinths blossom and on the brink irises are reflected in the glassy water, rippled now and then by the serene passage of a swan. Ducks go bottom up under a willow like Rapunzel's hair. The broad back of a carp glides by like a leisurely torpedo...I'm sure I've seen such perfectly gardened water somewhere. But not, alas, in my garden.

The waterfowl, for a start, eat the plants that are supposed to be oxygenating the water. Egbert and Percy, our swan and her mate – the names are interchangeable – made short work of gobbling every bit of the water-lilies I planted. Irises, pickerel weed, duckweed, bogbean are all one to them. The ducks are equally omniverous. (The only plant they spurn, and hence the bane of our lives, is blanket weed: I fantasize about a submarine loom that would weave it into bedclothes for mermaids.)

Without the benefit of oxygen from plants the pretty fish I stocked the pond with have mostly, it seems, succumbed. Not the carp, though: the great brutes (some are 15 years old now, and weigh as many pounds) thrive on a diet of the mud they constantly churn up from the shallows. We do catch occasional glimpses of gigantic gold-fish in the murk – they are, after all, I'm told, only fashion-conscious carp. Our pond-picture, in brief, falls short of the ideal.

Turning for help to that excellent gardener Frances Perry, in her classic *Water Gardening*, I find with dismay no reference at all to water-fowl. Can it be as simple as that: a choice between ducks and a balanced pond? It depends, you will say, on the depth of the water and on its flow (only ours doesn't). I also suspect it depends on the amount of nitrate neighbouring farmers chuck on their fields.

The search for balance, compromise, serenity, clean water etc still goes on. None too soon, it seems, I am calling in expert advice. You can expect to read more on this stressful topic in due course.

—June—

THE BEATEN TRACK

Having battled her way last autumn from Lhasa to Kathmandu, combining geology with a spot of seed collecting, our Member Peigi Wallace was intrigued to find a shop called Annapurna Seeds (Regd.), whose sign proclaimed it another 'member: Royal Hort. Society: London'. I have Peigi Wallace's photograph of it here. It scarcely seems worth the taxing trek from Lhasa. The plants painted on the sign are, as far as I can work out, a lettuce, a cauliflower, two carrots and two parsnips.

—July—

LABOUR DAY

May Day in Greece. I have never seen such a profusion of wild flowers, nor so many people picking them. We picnicked out on the plain of Marathon, in an olive grove more brilliant with colour than any Renoir orchard.

Next door a farmer was weeding a field of broad beans. I picked through a heap of weeds he had pulled up: Aphrodite's scarlet poppy and the yellow-horned one with blue-grey leaves, sky-blue lupins with a white stripe, pink mallow, white rocket, deep purple *Lavandula stoechas*, bundles of orange-yellow *Chrysanthemum segetum*, an oxalis with yellow flowers two inches across, silk-pink convolvulus, pale blue lovage and royal-blue *Anchusa*, low-growing purple echiums, various striking thistles, mullein and yarrow, valerian and bright-magenta gladioli. Many-coloured vetch scrambled through everything. Cistus, both pink and white, were blooming in the rocky road between the fields. A dense thicket of broom caught my eye by glinting like satin in the sun: *Genista cinerea*. Is this most graceful of brooms an Athenian citizen as well?

There were other picnickers in our olive grove, too, complete with a very fragrant barbecue. But then it was hard to find a corner of Attica that day without a family out garnering armfuls of flowers and plaiting them into wreaths. The wreaths were to adorn their motorcars, which took on the appearance of a sort of traffic jam of family shrines on the road back to Athens in the evening. Radiators, windscreen wipers, aerials, all were wreathed with sadly drooping flowers. 'It's the only day of the year Greeks look at wild flowers at all', said our host.

One image I recall as almost magical, crossing the Pendeli hills in the evening light: the low sun shining through the pine woods and catching the pale bells of thousands of asphodels under the trees.

— *August* —

PLANTS IN THE WRONG PLACE

Walkers about Westminster have recently found themselves side-stepping a large number of unexpected wooden obstacles on the already cluttered pavements. The City Council has parked massive 'planters' among the meters along, among other thoroughfares, Pall Mall and St James's Street. On the face of it it sounds a reasonable idea; to install a spot of horticulture rarely does any harm. On closer inspection, however, something has gone very wrong. The proprieties of design are being flouted. There is neither appropriateness, harmony nor unity in what the Council has done.

Pall Mall and St James's Street are not avenues. Nor for that matter is Piccadilly. They could be, but as far as I know they never have been, and their essential nature is urban and un-treed.

Were they to be avenues, their trees should be planes, the traditional London tree for 200 years, and the trees should be planted in the ground to grow tall.

But what has the Westminster City Council done? It has dumped its planters, tall unpainted wooden boxes at that, in well-spaced pairs seemingly wherever there is a plain piece of pavement and any room to stroll along.

In them it has planted a woefully misconceived selection of trees and shrubs. Each has a principal tree. Some are appropriate (or at least growable); no harm should come to a ginkgo or a *Sorbus*. Others are laughable. Outside the RAC there are what seem to be golden thujas – and Brooks's Club has been given, of all things, Christmas trees. Conifers will not survive in a city street, and their lingering deaths will be a most unpleasant sight.

Worse still, around this ill-matched un-avenue, the Council has been generous with a gallimaufry of shrubs. 'Tough' shrubs, you understand, that should survive, if not actually grow, in this hell-for-plants of a city street. But a mixed bag, in each planter, of different habits, and colours, and growth rates: cotoneaster, spiraea, pyracantha, senecio, vinca and euonymus.

If they do grow, they will obstruct the pavement even more with a dog's breakfast of ill-considered and irrelevant colours and shapes. If they don't (and I fear there are some who will make sure of this) the Council will have a chance to think again.

— September —

IF THIS WERE *MY* GARDEN

To Wisley the other day to see how the garden was surviving the soaking spring. As always, good order and surprisingly little sign of wear from the thousands of feet that could easily, one would think, churn the green walks into bogs.

It is always the business-like, working areas of Wisley that I enjoy most. The trial grounds like a military exercise; the vegetables, the hedge demonstrations and above all the fruitground and the plots where rootstocks are on trial and ingenious modes of pruning are being practised.

It is Wisley's misfortune that it has no house to relate to in a domestic way, hence no individual owner whose imagination, and quirks and foibles too, it can reflect. Up to a point, horticulture can span all tastes, and at that point Wisley has to stop.

Does everybody, I wonder, say to himself, 'Now if this were *my* garden there would be a fountain here, or a bed of pansies there'? This spring I was saying to myself I would build some handsome pavilions to keep dry in. The Japanese have lots of rain, too. But they turn it into an entertainment. They take pleasure in their spouting gutters and bending bamboos from a snug vantage point on the fragrant matting of a tea-house.

The Sublime Tuber

There is one branch of horticulture which as far as I know is completely neglected in this country, and that is the culture of the truffle. (You may agree that truffles are not found in gardens, and that they are thereby excluded from horticulture. But would we not cultivate them in gardens if we knew how?)

One-hundred-and-fifty years ago (September 1837) *The Gardener's Magazine* carried a very complete article on truffles, how to find them and how to cultivate them. The instructions are given in detail and with such confidence that it is hard to believe that they were not effective. Yet the truffle remains as rare as it ever was.

The subject is worth more diligent research. I shall keep my ears open. Indeed I will follow the instructions and let you know what (if anything) happens. Provided you promise to do the same for me.

—October—

Season of Mists

Four influential nurseries are campaigning at present to encourage us to plant more plants in autumn. They are, they explain, rushed off their feet in spring. Autumn is the season of the well-pondered choice, with time for careful planting. And if you get your plants in while the soil is still warm they will put on root growth before winter dormancy sets in. So they will be under less stress when spring comes.

I have always been an advocate of autumn planting. For one thing it is so much easier to be realistic about whether (or where) there is some space for a new plant when the present residents have all their top-hamper.

But whereas spring here in Essex used to be so dry that autumn was automatically first choice, recent seasons have made such considerations redundant. The whole of this rain-sodden summer has been a most ideal planting season.

De Gustibus

Of all the gardening books that came my way last year, I think the one that gave me the most pleasure was Horace Walpole's *Essay on Modern Gardening*, originally of 1771, reissued in a handsome new edition by the Stourton Press.

Walpole's easy, lucid, slightly mocking style is always a pleasure to read. But what struck me most on reading his account of garden history was the fundamental difference in his attitude to the past and our own.

Today it seems to be the convention of scholarship to be reverential. We have societies to preserve and promote the memory of almost every period and phase of taste. A generation ago Georgian was in, Victorian was out. Now Victorian is in with a vengeance – but so is Edwardian, between-the-wars, '50s, '60s...And the same is true looking further backwards. Is anything out of fashion today? Tudor perhaps? Not a bit. Look at all the new knot-gardens.

In England's Augustan Age (for so the later Georgians liked to style their time) the past was for making fun of. Walpole dismissed the hanging gardens of Babylon as 'triffling, of no extent, as a wanton instance of expertise and labour'. Pliny, he said, 'delighted in what the mob now scarce admire in a college garden'. In Kip's views of the seats of our nobility and gentry in about 1700, 'we see the same tiresome and returning uniformity'.

It was the taste of his day that Walpole celebrated. But then there was a prodigious lot of taste to celebrate.

1988

—January—

AFTERMATH

The ill wind of 16 October is not going to be forgotten for a very long time. Long after this generation of gardeners has gone to paradise October 1987 will remain a significant date in garden history: the date that removed so many living monuments from our gardens, parks and the countryside.

Each person has his own tale to tell. Mine is of a miraculous near miss, when our best Scots pine, a monster that had seen plenty of service, beautiful in its decay but already condemned and awaiting the surgeon's saw, was blown with infinite precision into the only place it could possibly have landed without causing harm and danger. There was not an inch to spare but plenty to be thankful for.

And of course the proverb has been proved right: good has come out of the storm, in the form of commitment and determination.

I am told that English Heritage was on the point of disbanding the gardens committee that has done such excellent work in listing 'heritage' gardens county by county. At the hastily called meeting to discuss the storm damage the committee was seen in a new light and reprieved. Indeed English Heritage has now made the very welcome appointment of the landscape architect David Jacques as its full-time Gardens Inspector.

The Countryside Commission, charged by the government with the task of repairing damage and restoring landscape features lost in both country and town, immediately formed a Tree Task Force, with £2.75 million to spend within the year. Conversation with its officers has convinced me that they are fully determined to make the best of the disaster by learning as much from it as possible.

The work ahead to repair the ravages of a mere four hours will take not months, but years. And yet it is extraordinary how rapidly the eye adjusts to the absence of a feature that it was accustomed to.

Our cedar of Lebanon (a 40-foot stripling) was blown flat. Within a few days I could look out of the window and accept its absence as natural. Then my kindly farmer-neighbour put it on its foot again, using a great deal of ingenuity and two enormous loaders.

Now it is the guy wires I am getting used to. Whether it will 'take' again I'm not at all sure. But one has to try.

TUBERS IN BATH

Nothing to report yet about my truffle-trials, but a most intriguing outbreak of truffle-finds reported by the *Bath and West Evening Chronicle*. In September the peculiar behaviour of squirrels led the owner of a garden in Bath to what is apparently a small but steady crop.

In October a council worker was clearing leaves in the grounds of an old people's home at Mount Beacon when he came upon a mighty fine specimen, the size of his fist.

Might they, I wonder, have been planted in the days of faith in these things? Or is Bath to become the capital of an English Périgord? (It has chefs who would know what to do about it.)

—February—

BEYOND COMPEAR

I never ate a better pear than one I had halfway up Mount Vesuvius in August. In appearance it was so perfect that it might almost have been made of china, like the fruit bowl. It was of medium size, the very model for the term 'pear-shaped', and a smooth, un-russet green.

Its flavour, sweetness and slightly crunchy texture all provoked exclamations of delight. But nobody knew its name. Everything, they said, that grows on the lava of Vesuvius grows in perfect health. All the fruit and veg there is sublime. Do I need a volcano in my garden to grow this wondrous fruit?

—April—

PARLEMENT OF FOWLES

I'm afraid the bullfinches have made the decision for me. The early-flowering cherries I planted to bring colour into our woodland glades with the bulbs will have to go. Having provided perfect cover for the finches, and masses of the buds they relish most, I can only watch help-lessly as the birds flash their little white rumps from tree to tree, leaving the ground covered with the scales of demolished buds.

On the evidence of this garden, bullfinches love seclusion. They are jumpy birds, with quite astonishing eyesight.

Not to be able to grow *Prunus subhirtella* 'Autumnalis' (in its white-flowered form, one of the prettiest of all trees in winter) is bad enough. One can, after all, see how the birds are tempted by its little buds swelling in December. But I'm afraid the list goes on and on. 'Kursar', that marvellous pink production of 'Cherry Ingram's', is out. So is the ravishing pink-and-red crab, *Malus floribunda*. And so is the bigger-budded and later superstar of cherries, *Prunus sargentii* (although I will keep it for its early-autumn blaze of red), and even the double-flowered gean, which is reduced here to a miserable few flowers on the tips of its twigs, instead of being a cumulus cloud of white all over.

Amelanchiers suffer the same fate. So do some apple trees. (I can't work out the bullfinch policy on apples.) The only exceptions seem to be such later-flowering cherries as 'Tai Haku' and 'Shirofugen'.

I am, in fact, paying the price for seclusion. There are no bullfinches on bypasses, or even, it seems, on suburban streets. So what I will do is to move all the flowering trees that are still transportable and put them right by the road, where passers-by can enjoy them through their windscreens – as I in turn enjoy their cherries.

—June—

UNDER GLASS

I promised (threatened?) to report from time to time on progress in the conservatory here. It has been part of our lives for over seven years now, and each year only adds to the delight it gives us. Particularly in the spring – and particularly this spring, so astonishingly balmy that the jasmine that usually waits until April was making the air heady with perfume by the middle of February. There is such excitement in its masses of pointed pink buds, lunging forward from the wall and pressing up to the glass, that *Jasminum polyanthum*, along with the plumbago in summer, is surely the most essential of all conservatory climbers.

At present there is a specially pleasing combination of colours under this showerbath of perfume. On one side of the garden door stands the Australian mint bush, *Prostanthera rotundifolia*, a cloud of tiny lilac bells. On the other stands a rhododendron that I think is *R. moupinense*, its leaves fresh apple green and its funnel-shaped, gently fragrant flowers a colour I can only call brick-rose.

Forming a perfect triad with these two colours are the sharp pale orange umbels of a big pot of clivia. And adding a sort of bass note in the spectrum are the soft spikes of deepest, most royal-blue-purple of a tall, sprawling *Salvia guaranitica*, the very same that the kind Michael Hickson gave me at Knightshayes to furnish the conservatory when it was all bare white bars.

Masses of green is essential, of course, to set off such a range of colours. It comes from camellia leaves, eucalyptus, ferns and bamboos as well as the flowers themselves. Among the foliage the strange little dodonaea, a slightly built tree with narrow sticky leaves of sombre red (and later little elm-like seeds), provides an unstartling contrast.

I wish I could say the orange and lemon trees in their pots made a proper contribution to the greenery. Alas, they do not. Nothing I can think of prevents them looking wan and chlorotic: a silent reproach among a crowd of friends. Reproach for what?

The tank in the conservatory is the only place in the garden which can be pretty well guaranteed heron-free and thus a safe place to let goldfish frolic. It is not big enough for any more flashy fish (nor do goldfish grow much beyond tiddler size in it). But all attempts at anything eye-catching in ponds outside are doomed by the big slow-flying fishermen. So at least the goldfish have nice warm water, and I a snug vantage point to watch them from.

—July—

TRUFFLE HOUND

My correspondence on this subject becomes more intriguing every week. We have established that black truffles are not exactly rare (although they are rarely exploited) in parts of Britain. Now comes the turn of the white.

Those who have been in the Langhe hills of Piemonte in November will not forget the astonishing pungency of the knobbly marbled cream and brown fungus that restaurants shave into crunchy slivers over pools of eggy *fonduta*. For impact, if not subtlety, the white truffle leaves the black one far behind.

A correspondent in Harrogate has what sounds like a proper plantation of them in the garden in association with, surprisingly, mature lime trees. She described the flavour as being 'like a young, milky walnut'. Slugs rush to the spot and eat most of the crop. From her account they do not sound so smelly as the Italian variety (which is also abundant in Tuscany). I will continue to delve.

NEEDLE POINT

Perhaps the single thing that I learnt most forcibly as a result of last October's famous storm was the real role of the forest floor in sustaining its trees. I was visiting an estate at Bignor in Sussex where (amongst many calamities) a whole wood of mature larches had been flattened. When we came to examine the rootplates (in no way could they be described as rootballs) we found that their maximum depth was no more than four inches. An 80-foot larch was supported and nourished entirely by a disc, some 12 feet in diameter but only wafer-thin in proportion, with absolutely no 'droppers' (as they call descending roots) at all. In fact the space below the tree had something of the look of a night club dance floor; a completely smooth clean circle of (in this case) pure white sand.

If anything is clear evidence of the virtues of mulch it is this. Without the fallen leaves of the forest, and the moss that stabilizes them, this would have been as barren as a beach. But just three or four inches of vegetable matter were enough to sustain a tree weighing several tons. With nothing but sand below you would think that a drought year would use up any water supply in such a meagre carpet.

A funny word, mulch. Where does it come from? I believe *Molsch* is the answer: a German dialect word meaning soft and beginning to decay.

—September—

BUFFON BETRAYED

To Paris, to the Jardin des Plantes, on a summer day of spring quality. Pearly light along the Seine clearing to Impressionists' sunlight, still cool in the shadows.

The Jardin des Plantes is older than Kew and scarcely less historic. As the Jardin du Roi it saw the introduction of many of the same plants as Kew in the eighteenth century.

In scope and layout there is no comparison with Kew. Order beds make a neat pattern down one wide *allée* of pleached plane trees. The trees and shrubs scattered among their herbaceous relations add interest, but a less than orderly effect. One of them I noted as particularly striking was *Firmiana simplex* among the *Sterculiaceae*, with huge soft deep-lobed leaves like a very exotic maple. Bean's *Trees & Shrubs* rules it out for south-east England on grounds of tenderness. One thinks of Paris as having much the same climate as London, but its slightly warmer continental ripening season may make the necessary difference between the two.

To go into the 'rock garden' we were stung for 11 francs each by a surprisingly modish maiden in a sentry box. I can see why people pay: it is the 'English' part of the gardens; a very pretty muddle of plants and trees in a dell with a token showing of alpines on rocky outcrops.

There is a large and curious weeping hornbeam whose label describes it as a '*Charme pleureur*': one pictures strong men reaching for their handkerchiefs. I was also rather intrigued by the French label (seen all over the gardens) of something I suppose must be a *Pelusia* in Latin. I can't find *Pelusiaceae* in the *RHS Dictionary*, but the species *Pelouse interdite* must have been widely planted at some time. There's nothing but bare lawn to be seen now.

Correct dress in the rock garden, by the way, is bathing suits. There are enough high-powered sprinklers to catch you however nippy you are. Is this, perhaps, the justification for the 11-francs entry fee?

The main purpose of our visit was to see the exhibition for the bicentenary of the death of Buffon, compiler of the *Histoire Naturelle* and superintendent of the Jardin du Roi for 50 years. It was shut. Instead we made a pilgrimage to his 'Gloriette', a gazebo made (most beautifully) in the forges which the polymath Buffon started near his home at Montbard in northern Burgundy, and the first iron building ever put up in France – the year before the Revolution.

It crowns the Labyrinth, which sadly I must report is now in total disarray. Sycamore, elder, brambles and nettles have practically swallowed up Buffon's memorial, and totally obscured the view from the top. *That* would never happen at Kew.

SITUATION VACANT

A historian friend researching in the Essex county archives has sent me an advertisement I can't resist reprinting: 'A Working Gardener who is Master of the Scythe and Knife, and can raise Cucumbers. Any person, whose moral character is unexceptionable, and who is industrious, sober, civil and of sufficient Ability will meet with good Encouragement'. The date is 9 November, 1764. The garden in question is Trad's own. (The post has now been filled.)

— *October* —

MSTAKE

It has been pointed out to me by a sharp-eyed reader that two totally different plants are referred to as 'Black-eyed Susan'. It's true. Rudbeckias and thunbergias, both yellow flowers with black centres, are frequently given the same common name. But why Susan?

Presumably the reference goes back to Sweet William's 'Farewell' in *The Beggar's Opera*:

All in the Downs the fleet was moor'd,
The Streamers waving in the wind,
When Black-ey'd Susan came aboard

– in which case, editors please note, the correct spelling (of ey'd) is with an apostrophe.

Odd, though, that the hero of that lyric also shares his name with a flower. And more confusing still the poet's line:

Adieu, she cries! and wav'd her lily hand.

If, as it seems, Gay was a better poet than a botanist, he was probably confused himself about whether it was Miss Rudbeck or Miss Thunberg to whom he was referring.

THE ITALIAN CONNECTION

Old timers will have little difficulty in recalling my repeated bitter complaints about the neglect of the once great Hanbury Gardens at La Mortola by the Italian authorities, and specifically by the University of Genoa, into the brown fingers of whose botany department the responsibility for the gardens had most unhappily fallen.

The letters I have had from people who have visited the gardens recently confirm that there is still much to enjoy in their uniquely dramatic site, and what is left of their architecture; even if their formal name, ll Giardino Botanico Hanbury, has become a mockery.

There is now once again serious hope that a new arrangement can be made, placing this horticultural treasure in the hands of a body worthy of it, and committed to its real restoration. The question is, as the coded phraseology goes, in the hands of the highest authorities. Pretty close to the summit, in fact. It is encouraging news.

But with it comes a rumour – I hope it is no more than that – that another equally remarkable Anglo-Italian garden has a problem. Ninfa, to those who know it, is a place of unique and haunting beauty; a ruined medieval walled city not far south of Rome, whose owners planted it as a wildly romantic English garden in the years after the First World War.

The special glory of Ninfa is its river, the Nymphaeus, a deep cold torrent which gushes from the cliff that rears up hundreds of feet above the extraordinary garden-town. In the garden its waters are conjured into all sorts of pretty games. They are also, of course, essential for the cultivation of a huge range of plants.

The problem is water extraction for intensive farming by new neighbours, who are raising kiwis and other fruit and vegetables alongside. There is a struggle for the river which could eventually be fatal for Ninfa.

Italy, so celebrated for the design of her gardens, is generally lamentably lax about their upkeep. It seems that plantsmanship is not a part of the Italian genius. Which makes it all the more vital that such rare examples of Anglo-Italian inspiration as Ninfa and La Mortola are protected.

—November—

VERY SHORT LIST

Of how many plants can you say that they are essential to a garden: that without them the sensations proper to a season are incomplete? Very few, it seems to me. A roseless garden would be a dreadful pity, but there are other plants that could distract you from their absence. I would sadly miss snowdrops and hellebores, daffodils and crown imperials, box, vines, clematis, hydrangeas...there is an infinitely extendable list of things I love to see in their places.

But the *sine qua non* is tobacco. The modest tobacco plant, standing around looking rather spare all day, blesses the evening air with a perfume sweeter than jasmine, more evocative even than honeysuckle.

This year we grew some varieties of the ancient favourite which have added to the garden in quite different ways. The six-foot *Nicotiana sylvestris* boasts jungly great leaves and lights up at dusk with wide white flowers somehow more richly, if less dramatically, scented than the 'ordinary' *Nicotiana alata*.

I have been enchanted, too, by the much more tentative-looking *Nicotiana langsdorffii*, whose little nodding flowers W.S. Gilbert would probably have called greenery-yallery.

Several little clumps of two or three plants have been tucked in among lower-growing hostas, lady's mantle, epimediums and such along a border where their profiles keep catching my eye.

LE PATRIMOINE

If the definition of a weed is a plant in the wrong place, then what is the definition of a 'planter', the device urban authorities use for putting plants where no plants should be – or inappropriate plants where a tree in the ground might have been a good idea?

I am not now talking of Westminster, whose city government has wisely taken the hint and removed most of the unfortunate wooden boxes it parked on its pavements last spring. More than anywhere it is the cities, towns and villages of France I am thinking of.

Nobody seems to be able or willing to stop house-proud *maires* with as much aesthetic sense as a croissant from tearing up the *pavé* in the oldest parts of town and replacing it with multi-coloured patio paving, incorporating elaborate and dreadfully permanent plant boxes. You weave your way to the *charcuterie* through a forest of cannas, and find a cotoneaster barring your way to the bank.

Everywhere ribbed concrete tubs are stuck against respectable old shop fronts and filled with riots of colour. Buildings and plants are both desecrated by the association. Can no one feel the impropriety of confusing a commercial street and a public park?

AT THE SINK

You expect your eyes to water when you peel an onion, but have you found yourself coughing when you scrape a potato? Is there some irritating principle in the skin of potatoes (new ones especially)?

—*December*—

REVIEW

The eye is a lazy instrument, easily made complacent by familiarity. Change in the garden has its own value, simply in making us see with fresh vision. Of course this is why we love the changing seasons so much; they bring events on to the stage and reawaken our interest in the familiar scene. (I wonder what it is like to garden in the tropics, where only more or less rain marks out the season. Pretty enervating, I shouldn't wonder.)

These thoughts were provoked by a bout of clearing in a part of the garden that had become routine. It was prefaced by several weeks of stalking – which is what I feel I'm doing when I try to creep up on different views at different times of day to re-estimate their effectiveness.

I always feel that revelation will come if I catch some aspect of a shrub, a border, a pond, unawares. If you surprise me prone behind a bush, or peering round a barn, that will be my excuse anyway.

It is often difficult to reconcile extreme aspects of a view: its winter and summer dress for example. Surveyed in winter, it calls for more evergreens; in summer, for less. The right compromise can take a lot of stalking.

Like many (perhaps most) gardeners breaking new ground, ten years ago I planted Leyland cypresses for shelter and screening.

Nothing could have been more effective; they could hardly do this job quicker if they were inflatable.

A good part of my current work is simply serving redundancy notices on what were only taken on as temporary staff in the first place – not just Leylands, but laurels, willow...everything whose principal virtue is speed.

The new prospects opened by their removal are like wonderful presents. To feel the light rushing in to claim the space when they come down is gloriously stimulating. Provided, that is, that I have done a thorough stalking job beforehand.

RED BRIGADE

Red is surely the hardest colour to blend into a harmonious garden picture. It is at its best in the confident masses of autumn leaves. Guardsman-fashion, all on its own as tulips or pelargoniums on the lawns facing Buckingham Palace, it has a definite ceremonial quality. But I confess that I have never liked the red borders at Hidcote (the only ones that I can think of). Pink would be fine, orange dandy, but full-blooded red somehow falls flat. Perhaps it absorbs too much light.

Now to admit that I have just been gazing at a combination of reds which pleased me greatly. The most striking feature is the dusky scarlet of 'Grayswood', a hydrangea that slowly takes on this wonderful old-master colour as the flowers mature. All mixed up with the hydrangeas are bushes of *Viburnum opulus* 'Compactum' covered with scarlet berries. *Tropaeolum speciosum* is insinuating its scarlet trophies into the picture and a Virginia creeper is beginning to add red leaves. I see nothing to object to there.

1989

—January—

WHO WEEDS THE ALPS?

I don't ski any more these days (not that I ever did very much), but the sight of thousands setting off to queue in the snow for *télécabines* at this time of the year reminds me of the magical holiday we had last summer in an alpine village that never gets crowded: that seems, in fact, to exist in that bygone age before package tours were ever invented. Its name is Champex.

Eager alpinists (gardeners as well as climbers) may indeed have heard of it, for it has that rare thing: an alpine garden in an alpine setting – and a big one, too. I had been there three or four times, once to ski, more often to walk and botanize in a dreamy sort of way, before I learnt that the garden was just up the street, and open (free) every day except Sunday and Monday.

I have not met the owner, who I'm told is Italian, but he is both a philanthropist and an artist. Around two of the most beautiful old carved and painted chalets I have ever seen, dominating a view of lake and forest, nearby peaks and distant perpetual snow, he has assembled a collection of it seems almost everything that does, or will, flourish at 5,000 feet.

It is a brave thing to do because he puts himself in direct competition with some of the world's loveliest wilderness. In June you wade through wild flowers in every meadow. In August we found ourselves picnicking by a torrent in an airy forest of ancient Arolla pines and gnarled and mossy larches, unable to sit without squashing a clump of the harebells that stain the mountain blue.

The sensation of being in a natural garden is astonishing: the feeling of controlled variety, with maybe 50 or 60 species of plant, none dominant, each repeated just often enough to be significant in the picture – and not a single thing, not a blade of grass, that could be described as superfluous or in the wrong place.

Who weeds the Alps? How does this perfect balance sustain itself? And where, you are about to ask, is this mountain paradise?

It is perched in its own valley high above Martigny and the road to the St Bernard Pass; on the eastern shoulder, as it were, of the Mont Blanc Massif. Its chalets cluster round its lake with an air of remote tranquillity that haunts me even as I write.

—*February*—

PARIS FASHION

The rage for conservatories has gone too far. Now the French government, fanatically trendy as ever, has plonked down three pyramidal ones, a mother and two pups, right in front of the main façade of the Louvre facing the Tuileries gardens.

Conservatories, at least, is what they appear to be. Why else give oneself the problem of cleaning all that glass? By way of justification (there can be no other) their design is attributed to the superstar architect I.M. Pei – he who at this very moment is rupturing the famous skyline of Hong Kong's Peak with a building for the Bank of China almost twice as tall as any of its neighbours. If you want a symbol of the vanity of governments, consult a specialist.

KITCHEN SINK

Reactions to my question about scraping potatoes (why does it make me cough?) have ranged from concern about my allergies to advice not to do anything of the kind in the first place but to eat the potatoes skins and all.

The consensus seems to be that it makes hay-fever sufferers sneeze (not cough), and that there is a connection between potatoes and asthma. Sometimes.

—*March*—

MOSS GARDEN

'Sintra's glorious Eden' was Byron's description of the sylvan hill that stands between the city of Lisbon and the Atlantic. The deep and winding way up to its bizarre Moorish palace on the summit is velvet-lined with moss. Sea mists enfold its giant trees. For a brief period, when Byron paid his visit, it was the very height of romantic fashion. That prince of folly builders, William Beckford, 'discovered' it, and rented the Gothic villa of Monserrate (to be near, it is said, to the Portuguese queen).

Beckford started an English garden in these romantic surroundings. More perfect gardening conditions can scarcely be imagined. This is almost the westernmost point in Europe, with no frost and warm Atlantic rains to keep plants growing all summer long.

The palace of Monserrate that stands today was built by another Englishman, Sir Francis Cook of Richmond, the first *Visconde de Montserrate*, a contemporary of Sir Thomas Hanbury who at the same time was making his great garden at La Mortola.

Similar conditions make the two gardens comparable in almost every way – including recent neglect. Both were at the height of their fame in the early years of this century. The Cooks even pinched the Hanbury's head gardener, Walter Oates.

The good news from Monserrate is that the *Camera Municipal* of Sintra is taking its horticultural heritage extremely seriously. It has called on Allen Paterson, former Director of the Chelsea Physic Garden, now Director of the Royal Botanical Gardens of Ontario. Ontario has responded generously, Canadian gardeners are now working alongside Portuguese. Restoration work is going apace. It sounds like a story heading for a happy ending.

– April –

TWOPENCE COLOURED

I'm sure we all feel a healthy pinch of scepticism when we leaf through the lurid pictures in nursery catalogues. The colours can often be relied on to tell you if a variety is red or white, but as between pink and white, let alone parchment and amber, that's asking a bit much.

A reader has sent me two catalogues which, interestingly enough, use the identical transparency of a group of bearded irises. You could be forgiven for not realizing it. The printers' interpretations (if that's the word) are so widely at variance that they could be different flowers altogether.

But more interesting are the nurserymens' opinions of their identities. What to Messrs Bakker of Holland are irises 'Red Vitifire', 'Good Hope', 'Speckless', 'Music Maker', 'AngelJoy', 'Flaming Dragon' and 'Pink Horizon', to their rivals, Groom's of Spalding, are respectively 'Ambassador', 'Bronze Charm', 'Empress of India', 'Golden Glow',

'Susan Bliss' and 'White Knight' (a variety, by the way, which appears to be either pale orange or somewhere between yellow and buff, depending on which printer you believe). Groom's, whose printing makes the lavender-blue 'Empress of India' look like an overripe aubergine, are marginally less purple in their prose style, but charge you another 10 pence a rhizome.

First Date

Why it has taken me nearly half a century to get round to visiting Egypt is a question I won't go into here. But the long overdue excursion has left a very deep impression. I still find I am having dreams about Horus and Osiris and Hathor. The least expected beauty, though, is perhaps the most enduring. I have become fascinated, almost obsessed, by palm trees: not as individuals so much as for the patterns of their groves.

On the deck of a Nile cruiser you are often at eye level with the palm-fringed banks, which move by as a mesmerizing frieze: fields and mosques, villages of buff and umber and blue houses, camels watering, buffalo ploughing, and everywhere Egyptians in their stately robes (only, alas, the children, or their mothers, have discovered bright fluorescent colours).

Date palms never grow very densely packed. Often they are multi-trunked, each trunk leaning out and curving up. All have the same thatch, but at different heights. They combine total monotony, in fact, with infinite variety: a wonderful design formula. I was reminded of an extraordinary Chinese scroll shown at the British Museum a few years ago which was nothing but daffodil (can that be right?) leaves, life-size, drawn in black ink and going on for yard after yard, never repeating, but never varying either.

Does the principle have a garden application? It is the kind of idea that should go on the back burner. Its time may come.

'Where Sweets Compacted Lie'

I believe in America they have a Box Society, or words to that effect – a group, that is, of people who admire the many merits of the genus *Buxus*. If there is one such in England it will be, I suspect, a pretty exclusive little clique.

Box is not something that clamours for attention. And yet (forgive me) it grows on you. I find that over the years – and it takes years – I have conceived a quiet crush on box. I plant it more and more.

Box is slow. But slowness is a virtue in small gardens, and box has three other virtues, at least. It seems almost indifferent as to light; it is perfect topiary material; and no rabbit that I have met will even take a sample nibble.

We already have box hedges, and 15 years ago planted what are now pyramids. Here and there in shady places we have substantial green puddings planted at the same time.

Box is back in my mind because I have just been refreshing a belt of trees (which mainly means dealing with dead and half-dead elms) by planting quite thickly a mixture of box and beech. Already in winter the green and brown are beautiful together. I think in spring the pale silkiness of the beech leaves with the almost Quaker plainness of the little round box leaves will be a joy. If the box survives the beeches' shade (and I'm sure it will) the long-term prospect – very long, I admit – is of the silvery columns of beech trunks rising from a rippling green foam.

THE DRIVE-IN ARBORETUM

At the end of last year I made an all too rare visit to Norfolk. Houghton, Holkham, Blickling, Felbrigg...there are many inducements to make the journey more often. But there is one compulsory stop for a self-confessed tree addict; indeed to any plantsman. Norfolk means first and foremost the indefatigable, encyclopedic, munificent Maurice Mason.

His are the only gardens (he has two, five miles apart, on totally different soils) that one customarily visits by car.

Maurice drives (at walking pace) through shrubbery, thicket and spinney, right up under the branches of trees so that he can check the label from the driving seat, and always bubbling away with an inimitable blend of deep knowledge and experience. To him (and his wife Margaret, whose knowledge seems to complement his precisely) there is as much to be said about any of their plants as about an old friend, warts and all.

'Really rather a nice bush, dear boy', says Maurice, driving me almost into the middle of a *Decaisnea fargesii*, about five yards across, its leaves straw yellow in the autumn sun. 'But the pods only stay blue for a week, and then it's pretty boring. Look at that *Catalpa fargesii duclouxii* over there: did you ever see such freshness? Always stays as green as a salad, dear boy, right up to the frosts; marvellous with the larches turning.'

WORD-ELDER

How many times do you read, in the gardening press, the expression 'this plant should be grown more often'...'not grown as often as it deserves' – or words to that effect? I know the feeling that drives scribblers to it . Why do most people persist in planting that endless lobelia, or forsythia, or those garish cherries, when we can show them so many more interesting, more original plants?

One answer may be that originality is not what the majority of gardeners look for; they would as soon be seen with a punk hair-do as with a plant of unorthodox appearance outside the front door. Another is that garden centres too often assume the above answer is the last word on the subject.

But might it not also be partly the fault of the writers themselves? What more boring and lame conclusion to a dithyramb about some marvel of creation, some flower of startling and original beauty, than to say 'should be grown more often' – when what you mean is uproot the laurels, make a bonfire of the privet, plant this jewel and adore it? Yet as a cliché it seems to have the power of ground elder.

Write out one hundred times after school: 'This line should be written less often.'

—*July*—

KITCHEN SINK

Few topics have brought Trad so many letters as new-potato wheeze. Here is a reader's explanation that I am ready to buy. The drug atropine is extracted from another member of the *Solanum* family: deadly nightshade. Atropine is used before a general anaesthetic to dry up secretions in the air passages and keep them clear. Is this clear?

— *August* —

SHEPHERD'S CALENDAR

I have always been haunted by the phrase in William Morris' memoirs, 'Whenever I smell hawthorn, I think of going to bed by daylight'. It so perfectly sums up childhood in midsummer in the country (as Walthamstow then was). His parents' handsome house now stands forlornly where the edge of Epping Forest used to be, surrounded by a suburbia that certainly started in the great man's lifetime. It was not only passing the house (which I do every time I go to London) but the impact of this year's hawthorn that set me thinking.

Hawthorn is widely known as 'May', besides its many other local names. ('Bread and cheese' is what they call it round these parts.) I looked it up in Geoffrey Grigson's *Englishman's Flora*, the standard work for folklore and gossip about our native plants. To my surprise he says that in the south of England it is regularly in blossom by 10 May. I say surprise, because this year's spring was surely at least two weeks early, and the hawthorn was only just starting to flower in the second week of May. My impression is that in our recent late springs it has flowered at the end of May and into June, which tallies more exactly with little Willy Morris going to bed by daylight. It is rash to set your watch by any plant's flowering, but perhaps someone keeps a record and can enlighten me.

LARNACY?

The strange blend of larceny and lunacy that leads people to steal plants would become almost as tedious a topic as football hooliganism if I mentioned it every time I hear about it. Perhaps horticultural hooliganism is the best way to classify it. Thieves have various euphemisms for their crimes. Nicking a cutting sounds almost like the proper gardener's jargon for something routine. It is, of course, plain thieving, for which the Koran has an appropriate penalty.

Most difficult to understand, for me at least, is the thief with real knowledge of a group of plants who steals not just the rarest, but sometimes even all the stock of some rare variety. It can hardly be for commercial gain: surely it is the sale-room, the actual functioning of the market, that gives Van Gogh such grotesque prices. No market; no price. One is forced back to a vision of the loony collector cackling fiendishly in his conservatory, his green-tinted specs steaming up with excitement at the thought that only he, he in all the world, can feast his piggy eyes on *Tradescantia tediosissima* 'Yawn'. When we catch you, and we will, the pillory is waiting. Stocks have far too fragrant associations for the likes of you.

—September—

ON THE PROWL

I imagine every gardener keeps a torch somewhere near the wellies and the trowels: there are times when close night-time inspection is essential, or at least great fun, and a distinct fascination about one's familiar plants lit by a single beam and casting random shadows on each other.

On summer nights I am usually still in the garden when the pub closes, waiting for the stillness that descends as the last car leaves the village: time to study the almost eerie whiteness of flowers that seize and hold the dying light. *Spiraea thunbergii* becomes a sheeted spectre in the gloom, and *Deutzia setchuenensis* – the queen of its tribe at any hour – in the gathering darkness becomes the vegetable answer to a halogen bulb.

Speaking of halogen bulbs, I am fooling with the idea of something a little more creative than a torch, but still a long way from digging up paths and laying cables. The scheme is a portable garden light that operates on stored solar power. I can picture the contraption: the golf trolley, with places for light, battery, bottle of Hock and four volumes of *Bean*. Happily it will be dark, so no one will see me.

— October—

THE TREE REGISTER

I hope Alan Mitchell will not take offence when I say that if I ever had a problem visualizing a prophet in full cry – Isaiah, for instance, or perhaps Elijah – I have only to think of him, preaching the power and beauty of trees, always coatless, regardless of the weather, his white hair blown about by the wind, on the slopes of Bedgebury Pinetum, or striding uncatchably through a Perthshire forest.

For 35 years, since he joined the Forestry Commission after service in the Fleet Air Army, Alan has visited, measured and recorded every remarkable tree in the British Isles – repeatedly.

His indefatigable forays have given him the basis for a practical and critical judgement of every species and variety, and how it grows in virtually every locality, which is without parallel. When Alan retired from the Forestry Commission in 1983 no one else was appointed to continue his unique form of research, but he and his colleague Victoria Hallett, who had been combining historical records back to the early nineteenth century for the complete biographies of the most notable trees, set up a consultancy practice together to give them the means to continue their work. Happily their records, and the work that goes into them, have now been given status of an educational charity, under the name of *The Tree Register of the British Isles*. At present it still takes the form of a card index. Their first priority is to put it on computer to provide much faster and easier access to its huge store of information.

Trees continue to grow and die. There will always be more work to be done keeping the records up to date, however amazingly complete they are: Alan Mitchell was able to give me the exact first flowering dates of hawthorns he had recorded over the last 35 years.

—November—

THE SOUNDING CATARACT

It was reassuring to snatch a visit to Scotland in August and be reminded of the qualities of rain. Ten days of it, after a baking July, had filled the burns and, at Crarae, had driven the torrent wild.

The sky was clearing for the evening respite when we stood word-less in the thunder of surely the most magnificent cascade in any garden. The river crashes from side to side in frenzy as it drops hundreds of feet among the rocks down to the shore of Loch Fyne.

There is something unspeakably touching, even obscurely grand, about the utter calmness of plants around a torrent. A Japanese maple stretched out a long bough of intricate leaves almost motionless, only inches above the infuriated water, like a patient priest in blessing. A lonely hypericum flower, an overgrown buttercup, hung on its frail stem weighed down with spray. Fern fronds reached up, and a pink ray from the west speared through the pines to light a tall eucryphia, a tower of wax-white flowers above the chasm.

Crarae and the splendours of its mountain slope were known to us. A new discovery, some 70 miles to the east in Perthshire, overlooking the Tay near Aberfeldy, was the quietly intimate garden of Cluny House. Now and then (luckily not too often) Trad finds himself in a garden which he knows will definitively change his perception of his own. Cluny is one of these. Needless to say it is a woodland garden, planted so close that if you walk around without constant scrutiny upwards, downwards and sideways, you will miss three-quarters of its beauties.

Late August is not exactly high season – at Cluny, packed with rhododendrons and Himalayan primulas, lilies and meconopsis, spring is the peak of flowering excitement – yet in woodland gardens, where seeds are ripening and leaves beginning to turn, August is the time of greatest fullness. Undistracted by crowding colours, the eye is free to wander and enjoy and the mind to store qualities of structure and mass and texture.

Not that colour was absent. Scarlet tropaeolum was invading the fading hydrangeas like a sharp attack of bindweed. What seized my imagination, though, about Cluny, was the sense of a private plants-man's world, or dream forest, where the élite among plants revel in each other's company.

ANTICIPATING GRAPES

A bunch of grapes has been ripening three yards from my nose all summer. Its incipient flower buds appeared, pressed against the window, in early June. Looking up from my desk I have watched as the canopy of vine leaves has become a bower of green and, in the sunlight, gold around the casement. In July the tiny buds, their formation anticipating the bunch of grapes to come, opened and the scent of the tiny creamy flowers came in elusive breaths through the open window, a reminder of the swooning sweetness of vineyards on midsummer evenings that accounts, they say, for so many Piscean children.

By August, the fertilized grapes were plain to see; almost like bigger flower buds still pressed against the glass. As sunlit day followed sunlit day, they began to enlarge imperceptibly, ever more luxuriantly embowered in leafy shoots that reached out two yards from the house wall. The panes set in their lead seemed to have been painted by Lalique in a kaleidoscope of greens and yellows, highlights and shadows, threaded with pink leaf-stalks and invaded from below by the vine-like leaves and elegant bud-sprays of Japanese anemones.

By late August the bunches had weight and pressed more urgently against the glass, while a magical metamorphosis turned their green quite suddenly, or so it seemed, to a pale *eau-de-nil* translucency. The sunlight was trapped in each globe as its sap began to sweeten.

They were already tempting to pick while they were still inedibly tart. Gradually they filled with sugar, as they had with light. On 12 September we harvested 15 bunches of 'Golden Chasselas', ripe but with that penetrating flavour that translates into excellent wine.

English winemakers should have an *annus mirabilis*. When fruit does really ripen in these northern parts its flavour is incomparable. The slowness of the process seems to build aromas and complex flavours that the South can never match.

INNOCENCE AND EXPERIENCE

This year there was even more surprise and delight than usual in the emergence from long-parched soil of the pale heralds of autumn, the colchicums. They are as simple and clumsy as anything newborn, these strange pink tulip flowers without stalks or accompanying leaves that fall over as soon as they have stood up.

How different are the next bulb flowers to spring from hiding: the intricate, highly wrought, brilliant-pink nerines. Beside the innocent colchicums they have the sparkling finish of a *poule de luxe*.

1990

—January—

TRAVEL SUPPLEMENT

I remember being transfixed by my first sight of Courances; not in the flesh, as it were, but in that beautiful picture book *Visions of Paradise* with photographs by Marina Schinz.

The picture was so close to my idea of paradise that for years I was reluctant to go and see for myself. The reality was bound to fall short of the image. Such crystal waters and emerald shades, such tranquil tree-reflecting pools, ducal in scale, mellowed by three centuries of stillness, should be visited only in dreams.

But Courances is real, and even lovelier than any photograph. What is more is that it is less than an hour south of Paris, just west of Fontainebleau.

For 130 years it has belonged to the family of the present owner, the Marquis de Ganay. The only illusion is that its past has been tranquil – or that its present is effortless. As the Marquis told me, it was a Luftwaffe headquarters during the Second World War, and then Montgomery's quarters when he commanded NATO for seven years after it at Fontainebleau. The Germans succeeded in blowing up part of one of the *allées* of plane trees, planted in 1782, that line the canals leading to the château, then, on leaving, fired a bomb dump in the park which destroyed most of the roof.

The principal effort in these calmer times is maintaining the waters in their crystal limpidity. Courances means 'running waters'; the park is fed by nine generous springs whose flow is directed into a dozen ponds, moats, canals and cascades. Keeping them free of weed is the job of voracious grass carp – so voracious that they quickly finish their salad and have to be netted out of one *pièce d'eau* and into another; their opportunity to have a snap at the Marquis and his gardeners.

The design of Courances is credited, without precise evidence, to the great Le Nôtre. It makes a fascinating excursion to compare its serene simplicity, just water, grass, trees and the odd statue, with the very much more emphatic grandeur of Vaux-le-Vicomte, half an hour away at Melun. Courances is a statement about peace, Vaux about power. But Vaux, behind its formidable façade, is also one of the most entrancing châteaux to visit, beautifully and ingeniously arranged by its owners, the de Vogüés, to tell its own story.

Between the two lies Fontainebleau with its strange forest full of rocky outcrops among the trees; an enchanted place to leave the Autoroute du Soleil on the way to or from the South.

—*March*—

RHODODENDYEN

I paid my second visit in December to the Wisley of Japan: the great new garden-cum-conservation area which is being developed in conjunction with the Society's newly formed Japanese branch.

It was a strange feeling to sit with an editor discussing the problems of translating *The Garden* into Japanese, halfway up a mountain covered with the deep green spires of cryptomerias. (The one part of the journal they never even try to translate, she assured me, is Tradescant's Diary.)

That the Society's first gardening enterprise overseas should be in Japan is largely due to the far-sightedness of the Treasurer. The owner is the Seibu Saison Group of stores, hotels and other enterprises; one of Japan's most prestigious business houses. That it will be a worthy one is beyond question: the Mount Akagi Nature Park, as it is called, is already a spectacle worth travelling a long way to see.

Specifically, once in Tokyo, you take the bullet train for 40 minutes to Takasaki on the northern (Niigata) line, change to a local train to Shibukawa, then hope some kind person will drive you up the mountain. Akagi is no Fujiyama, but a very substantial hill nonetheless. It was chosen for the project for its relative remoteness from the pollution of Tokyo and its surroundings, and its more or less natural woods, in which you would weep to see the maples and the magnolias, the stachyurus, the clethra and the callicarpa and the *Cornus controversa*, ornamenting a matrix of cryptomeria and a delicate oak they call *Quercus serrata*. Even the sere grasses of winter in Japan have the look of delicate decorations installed by some patient artist of the woods.

The nature park covers 120 hectares in all, of which about half is being left more or less wild, and half is being gardened on a spectacular scale. Work started in 1985.

On my first visit, in the spring of 1988, there were already passages of great beauty. I remember in particular a positive river of yellow and green hostas in all their May freshness cascading down a little ravine among rhododendrons and maples that already looked established – but for their incongruous rigging.

Rigging is even more a feature of Akagi today: rigging of giant bamboo scaffold poles, of wire cables and beautifully knotted ropes holding in place full-grown trees that have been moved around like chessmen, it seems as a matter of course.

In places it looks as though the whole forest has been playing musical chairs – and it is not only the trees that move: the dry bed of a torrent is lined with boulders that weigh up to 30 tons, all of them precisely placed by the sort of equipment that is usually seen on emergent motorways. In due course (when the pump is installed) a respectable river will appear.

In quiet contrast to this Jove-like activity, a plain little reedy pool in another part of the forest is accompanied by odd-looking tent-like structures equipped with lamps. This is the entomological department of the park, where the entomologist in charge showed me no less than 25 kinds of dragonflies that had been collected almost as soon as the pond was filled. Every butterfly and moth on Mount Akagi is being catalogued here. Birds, mammals (not many), and every creature will be similarly put on show and explained to a rising city-bred generation which thinks (as I was told) that a butter-fly is just another charming novelty from the design people of a department store.

An unexpected feeling of *déjà vu* came over me as I tramped admiringly round the woods which are designated for the rhodo-dendron collection. Where had I seen such a profusion of rare species, planted out with supreme confidence when they were only a few leaves high among perfectly chosen trees?

Then it struck me. Has James Russell been here? I asked. But, of course; Russell-san comes twice a year. He is our adviser on plant-ing. Brickell-san introduced him to us.

Ray Wood, the Russell masterpiece of woodland gardening at Castle Howard, looked just like this (though not half the size) ten or so years ago. No one else can conjure up an enchanted forest from scratch as he can. What a formidable combination: Russell plants-manship and Japanese engineering.

— April —

WINTER SUN

Is there any limit to the value of mahonias? I can't imagine why any garden does not have a clutch of these incomparable evergreen shrubs.

Trad went to Windsor, to the Savill Garden, home of the National Collection of Mahonias, to see the truly stunning *M. confusa* and *M. gracilipes*; at first sight two more additions to the must-have list. They were not on show, but the expedition was made infinitely worthwhile by those that were.

The Savill Garden is famous for its well-clothed look in winter. Rhododendrons and camellias furnish it fully even when trees and soil are bare. It was New Year's Day, drizzling and dire, yet great yellow mahonias were lighting even the darkest corners. The fierce fronds of 'Faith', 'Charity', 'Lionel Fortescue' and 'Winter Sun' are as dramatic as grappling irons in the garden at any time. Crowned with their explosions of yellow flowers they dominate the scene.

There are soft-contoured ones, too: the ordinary Oregon grape that flowers in spring, *M. aquifolium*, the glistening *M. undulata* and the severely matt but hugely flowery *M. rotundifolia*. *Mahonia pinnata* is a finely fretted little bush, and *M. nervosa* a suckering ground-coverer of almost fern-like character.

Sheltering on the cosseted tall south wall of the Savill Garden, I spotted *M. fremontii* from the American desert, pale blue leaved, as fine as filigree, and a clear reminder that the good Lord had only just finished his berberis designs when he hit on his mahonia masterplan.

— June —

GREENERY-YALLERY

My *cri de coeur* about the lemon-coloured leaves of the lemon trees at Château Trad met with an overwhelming response from far and near. What they need, most kind correspondents agree, is Epsom salts, watered in the pots and also sprayed on the leaves. The recipe, it seems is ½lb of Epsom salts in 2½ gallons of water for irrigation, and the same formula, with a dash of washing-up liquid, as foliar feed.

Oddly enough, two trees in pots which were seriously neglected in a shed last winter, and whose soil had dried out to the point where they were looking desperately shrivelled, are (before Epsom salt treatment) much greener than their more cossetted colleagues.

—*August*—

WEATHER MCFORECAST

I have a proposal for the BBC. It concerns the weather forecast. For far too long we have been subjected to 'experts' from the Met Office garbling the information we need, in place of professional broadcasters. A journalist is trained to put a story in order, make it clear and stick to the point. The rambling delivery of our broadcasting metpersons demands total concentration if one is to glean any hint of their views. An area of high (or low) pressure is often the clearest clue they let drop, before going on to their favourite theme, the 'risk' (never, for some reason, the hope) of rain in the Orkneys.

One can scarcely blame them, perhaps, for their natural preoccupation with the weather back home — except that 75 percent of the forecast tends to be dedicated to the regions where 10 percent of the population lives.

In contrast the shipping forecast is always a model of dispassionate organization and clarity. My proposal is straightforward: it consists of a weather report from garden stations exactly analogous to the coastal station reports offered to seamen. Thus at 5.55pm we should be told: 'Wisley' (or Harlow Carr, or Rosemoor, or Wye), 'light rain clearing, wind west, backing southerly 10-15 mph, daytime temperature 40-48°F, 40 percent chance of ground frost at night, broccoli delicious' — or whatever crisp titbit our weatherman had up his sleeve. He should use no parentheses, conditional phrases, inverted clauses or admit his nostalgia for Dundee. All we need to know could be expressed in a few seconds of pithy actuality. A pious hope.

—September—

HI HO, HI HO!

Speaking of ambitious projects, there is one which has been simmering steadily for several years now which Trad is fairly bursting to see. Walt Disney Inc., encouraged by the French government to a degree that would make you gasp and rub your eyes, is putting the finishing touches to Europe's first Disneyland almost at the gates of Paris.

The valley of the Marne may not seem to have much in common with southern California, Florida, or for that matter Tokyo – all places where the weather is generally congenial for an outing. But Disney's head gardener (scarcely the term, but Le Nôtre affected it too) has been doing his best to fool us. For the last five years he has been hunting up the most exotic-looking evergreens that stand a chance of surviving in the Isle de France. Expect forests of fatsias, groves of gum trees, and a little Patagonia of *Nothofagus dombeyi*.

Morgan 'Bill' Evans, now in his 80s, might have expected a less harsh posting. His father's nursery in Santa Monica was the supplier of plants to the stars when Beverly Hills was just emerging from the sage brush. Bill did Walt Disney's own first garden – and the thing sort of grew from there.

—October—

CIRCUS MAXIMUS

I occasionally wonder whether I am not overstressing the Japanese theme. It certainly crops up here more regularly than, say, notes from Spain or even Cornwall. The argument against is that relatively few of us are going to see the gardens of Japan; the argument for is that Japan is the one nation besides Britain which still actively practises a distinct national style of gardening with total conviction – and conspicuous success. Few of us are averse to Japanese electronics or cars. It makes no sense to close our minds to their horticulture, either.

Especially in the year of Osaka. Osaka, Japan's second city, has been holding, since April, the father and mother of Garden ('and Greenery') Festivals. Gateshead is a village fête in comparison.

Admittedly not all the 250 acres of the site are dedicated to horticulture; about a quarter is a 'City Area' of commercial exhibition halls and a 'Magical Crossroads' – code for a high-tech funfair.

Another quarter or so must be taken up by the streets, stations, restaurants and other facilities needed to cope with vast crowds. On the day I was there at ten in the morning, the people-meter by the gate told me that 119,638 had beaten me to it that day. The total gate is expected to be well over 20 million people.

The pious purpose of all this, according to the Commissioner General, is to 'contribute to a full appreciation of the relationship of gardens and greenery to human life, thus helping in the creation of a truly pleasant and mentally rich society for the twenty-first century.' Is 'mentally rich' the same as 'spiritually rich', I wonder?

Not surprisingly, by far the most impressive parts of the show are the Japanese ones – from the 'Valley of Flowers' which greets you at the entrance, to the dramatic conservatory which accommodates plants from environments as diverse as tropical rainforests and the Arctic.

The 'Valley of Flowers' is a serpentine path wandering through five acres or so of immaculate planting. In May, golden lilies in beds the length of cricket pitches shone in dappled light under birches, with not a single withered flower to be seen. Flitting among them in yellow overalls were the 'honey-bees' (so the backs of their overalls told us) whose job is to see that no flower is allowed to pass its prime.

Most impressive of all, though, is the Japanese Government garden; a display that summarizes the whole theme of the show, from forest ecology to a terrace of rice paddies, to flower arranging, to infrared aerial photographs of Japan and its cities to show how much (or how little) vegetation they have. One hypnotic exhibit is a robot propagator whose sanitised secateurs apparently guarantee virus-free cuttings. Beyond the plate glass is a grove of giant bamboos dappling a rocky cascade, and beyond them the pines, maples and the rest that form the starkly limited palette of the Japanese gardener – yet in a good gardener's hands somehow never seem stereotyped.

I'm afraid none of the 55 other national gardens comes close. Most are pretty perfunctory: the British contribution perhaps too ambitious (and too far from home). The Chinese pavilion on the brink of 'The Sea of Life' (the butt of many jokes; pollution from construction works killed all the fish) is marvellously elegant; the Dutch, next door, a mere bit of canal and a beer garden.

Will the 20 million be mentally enriched by this *Circus Maximus* of horticulture? Only if they are very selective – not to mention in good physical shape. Otherwise, I fear, they are more likely to be both physically and mentally exhausted.

—November—

UNDER THE GRILL

Even in 1976 our lawns never reached quite the toasted condition they were in by early August. Or perhaps the grass did, but we had so much clover then that there was still a shading of green here and there. Complete toasting has some curious side effects.

When you stop mowing, the deep-rooted weeds seize their advantage. We have a patch of yarrow in the grass I had never noticed which has raced up to flower – rather prettily, I think. Tree suckers that would have been knocked back by the mower come up with alarming vigour. I never thought of a horse chestnut as a suckering tree, but where one was felled by the January storms and its stump removed its roots are sending up lush foliage for rods, poles or perches around.

Shallow-rooted beeches and birches are a sad sight, but some plants which normally live on sufferance in our cool and cloudy climate have shown their appreciation of a good baking. The most surprising sight in the garden is a wisteria so covered in bloom and such salad-fresh leaves that it makes me cool just to look at it. Clambering up into it is that cucumber-cool clematis, *viticella* 'Alba Luxurians', whose sepals can't decide whether they are white petals or green leaves. The two climbers lower the temperature of their corner by 10°F.

— December—

THE YEAR OF THE RABBIT

Looking back over 1990, one of the best features of a year of such sustained sunshine was the splendid matinées and evening performances by so many roses. True the matinée of some was a bit short-lived in the torrid heat but, well and truly dead-headed, they were soon back.

One that has quite seduced me is the oddly named 'Alister Stella Gray', whose evolving tones of egg/honey/cream is the perfect foil for the powder-blue of *Ceanothus* 'Gloire de Versailles' and the almost identical colour but contrasting texture of *Clematis* 'Perle d'Azur'. 'A.S. Gray' went off like champagne at a Grand Prix in June, and by the end of August was at it again. Its scent is almost tropically sweet and heady.

Another rambler that this year has been in flower for as long as not is 'Phyllis Bide'. For me, very few roses get away successfully with the combination of yellow and pink or red (most notoriously not that hideous 'Masquerade'). 'Phyllis Bide' pulls it off in gentle yolk and salmon, fading to blushing ivory, in large clusters of complex small flowers. Graham Thomas finds them sweetly scented too, but I'm afraid his sense of smell is keener than mine.

The most galling feature of the year, apart from lack of water, was the resurgence of the rabbit. I had almost forgotten what a menace they can be – or how hard to shoot. They operate a system with the pigeons, who can tell a gun from any other implement at 200 yards. The pigeons get up, clattering away with a tremendous racket, and every little bunny pauses in his destruction of whatever you have failed to net and sits cutely for an instant on his hind legs, just long enough for the gunner to think he has a chance.

Every bunny, though, is an expert in calibres, chamber lengths and for all I know muzzle velocity. He knows the precise range of every gun. I can see him sniggering at my garden gun, a 410, as kids' stuff. Then as soon as I make a move he shows me his white end as he lol-lops into the ditch and away. My humane wish for 1991 is that rabbits may lose their taste for exotics and stick to good old grass. More to the point, that we have some grass in '91.

1991

—*February*—

HERE BE DRAGONS

A few years ago, Peter Hayden took a haunting photograph of a chinoiserie pavilion, framed in maple leaves and reflected in a rocky pool. It was the first intimation to the world at large of the existence of a forgotten masterpiece of Victorian gardening in the grounds of a Staffordshire hospital.

Peter Hayden was ringleader of the group of local enthusiasts determined to rescue and restore Biddulph Grange, one of the most exotic products of an age that was uninhibited in its taste for the romantic and bizarre. Fourteen years later their enthusiasm is about to be rewarded. The garden is being comprehensively restored by its new owners, the National Trust, and in May will open to the public for the first time in all its wonderful weirdness.

Trad paid a visit in November to see restoration work in full swing. Biddulph is one of those gardens whose plan makes it seem far bigger than its 15 acres. Its creators, the plantsman James Bateman and his friend the painter Edward Cooke, seem to have had that touch of megalomania essential to monumental garden making; they moved earth like McAlpines and winched prodigious boulders about as though they were shuffling cards to mould the glens, the grottoes and caverns that divide the garden into its far-fetched components.

You plunge into a Stygian tunnel to emerge into the enchanted glade that is 'China', have scarcely recovered when you are faced with a great gilded buffalo attended by dragons, and enter a homely little Cheshire cottage to find yourself face-to-face with a monstrous Egyptian idol.

This is the Disneyland aspect of Biddulph, and it leaves an indelible impression. But horticulturally there is more to it than just eccentric follies. Each part of the garden is a horticultural entity strongly coloured by its planting. Above all 'China', at the heart of the garden, manages to be a credible microcosm of China's flora. Many of its plants were given to Bateman by Fortune from his Chinese expeditions.

The National Trust has all the records to help it recreate the high-Victorian plantsmanship that made Biddulph one of the most important gardens of its time. This year's visitors will be able to see the process of garden-making using the precise materials of 150 years ago.

—March—

METRO-GOLDWYN-TRAD

I wonder how many gardeners have been seduced by the marvellously ingenious (though so dismally christened) little Camcorder. The idea of making movies of one's garden visits, and one's own gardening efforts, is certainly appealing – especially when you can play them on your TV set without any fuss. Trad, I'm afraid, has succumbed, and found himself not only a new hobby, but a new way of (literally) focusing on gardens.

The first thing my little machine taught me was a fresh respect for film cameramen. It is far from easy to achieve even something so seemingly simple as a steady pan from side to side. It certainly isn't the way your eyes naturally take in a scene. They (mine, anyway) usually start with the most attention-grabbing shape or colour, or indeed simply focus on whatever arouses my curiosity.

The video camera is good at this. The zoom lens indeed is almost too good at starting close up to a curious flower, then retreating to reveal its surroundings and the whole scene. Or doing the opposite, 'finding' some significant details of plant life in a wide shot and prowling up to it. The temptation to a novice cameraman is to zoom in and out far too much, forgetting that perhaps the most important function of the eye is to rest on something for long enough to give it a thorough examination.

Should I perhaps have stuck to my old still camera and tried to master that instead?

—April—

SAGE ADVICE

A Swedish correspondent, Erik Malm, who read my note on rabbits in the garden, has sent me his recipe for controlling roe deer, who started by making sorties into his garden from the nearby forest, but grew bolder and bolder until they 'are practically born in the garden'. Pretty though they are, they are too fond of flowers as fodder (rosebuds are a special favourite) to make ideal garden pets.

Mr Malm noticed that they never touched plants with aromatic leaves. So he experimented with a decoction of common sage in water, boiled for 15 minutes, which he put in a spray bottle and sprayed over the plants that roe deer preferred.

It worked, he says, like a charm. He was soon able to abandon drenching whole beds with his sage-water and just give a daily squirt or two here and there. The roe deer, it seems, have become like Ferdinand the bull: admirers, instead of consumers, of flowers.

—*June*—

COLD LIGHT OF NIGHT

One cold afternoon recently I started leafing through those tombstone-like volumes of *Gardens Old and New* published by *Country Life* just before the First World War (strangely no date appears in them). Well-printed black-and-white photographs have a power denied to colour: they scan the profile of a scene and the tones that compose it with a relentless, undistracted eye. They have a way of showing up ugliness in outline and spottiness in planting.

It is very easy to be repelled by the grandiose repetitions of late-Victorian gardening. Judging by many of the great houses illustrated William Robinson's influence still had a very long way to go. To be fair, though, the editors of *Country Life* and their photographer, Charles Latham, were seemingly more interested in architecture than plants: there are several mansions included whose gardens only scrape into the pictures at all because they lap up the walls of the house. Right over them many a towering gable is nothing but a dark green wedge of ivy.

I took advantage of the full moon that very night to go out and inspect my own garden in black and white to compare it with Mr Latham's photographs. Oh dear. Black and white is a tough test. All the faults of ugly outlines and spotty planting were brought home to me with a vengeance. Better to see the Edwardians through the indulgent (and probably flattering) eyes of George Elgood, Beatrice Parsons and the other watercolourists who washed their walks and borders in the haze of a golden afternoon.

1991

SELF-PROPELLED

I'd love to know how violets decide where they want to grow. And indeed how they get there. The garden here has pools of white violets scattered under the trees, almost all the same size, like a smallish table-cloth, and at fairly regular intervals – say 50 feet apart. No one owns up to having devised or procured this arrangement – and yet it spreads year by year. I would love some of the tablecloths to grow large enough to combine into a great sail, but something tells me I should not interfere.

—July—

THUG LILY

I suppose I should have realized when I planted it, at the bottom of a hole a full spade deep, a ceremony more like a burial, that alstroe-merias are no frivolous fancy, to be cast aside when the whim passes, as Bertie would say, like a worn-out glove. Alstroemerias are a com-mitment for life.

They operate in the bowels of the earth where they cannot be traced, invisible till April, then suddenly filling yards of ground with pale limp leaves, not just where they were interred, but in the middle of the Japanese anemones, up through box hedges, the other side of the path and even the other side of the wall.

In July friends beg for pieces of the flesh-tinted lily with its flashes of yellow, copper, coral and crimson. I offer them bindweed as a more controllable alternative, but they will not listen. Friends who come in August ask what that great bare patch, that scrofulous untilled ground, is doing in the middle of the border. It is where the sweet Peruvian lily shot up, smothered everything, and then as suddenly withdrew from sight, leaving as a reminder only its brown seedpods on their untidy leaning stems and the annual problem of what to do with the scorched earth. It is too late to sow annuals. This year I decided that shrubs could tough it out. I am waiting to see whether the *Viburnum carlesii* and the cistus I planted have survived their summer of treading water in the lily tidal wave.

—August—

BRIEF ENCOUNTER

Trad retreated in some disorder in May from his long-anticipated first visit to the Hindu Kush. Drunk (metaphorically; this is Islam, remember) with the wild beauty of the Bumberet Valley, where the Kalash tribe, reputed descendants of Alexander the Great's lost legion, lead a cheerfully pagan life among their sparkling torrents and giant walnut trees, Trad collided with a sharp outcrop of Kush and had to retire with a broken arm.

He was in the hills for just long enough, though, to have only one ambition: a speedy return to this most magnificently wild frontier. Quite apart from the fertile valleys and the desolate screes, the distant glimpses from the Chitral bazaar of perpetual ice on the shoulders of Tirich Mir, the Afghans with their turbans and Kalashnikovs, and the Pathans with their profiles and their no-holds-barred polo, the five-star attraction in May was the roses. It seemed one petal would perfume a room. In the old fort by the river in Chitral, ringed with crumbling cloisters of the Moghul kind and shaded by a Chennar tree the size of a mosque, a line of bushes stood wet with the overnight rain. Their flowers were soft, very double, small-petalled and a tender shade of lavender-mauve. But their scent had the sweetness of harems.

OLD SOLDIER

John Codrington's legion of friends have felt a mixture of bereavement and sad satisfaction since he died in April.

His departure became him as well as everything he did. He had reached the age of 93 and was finding life as rewarding as ever when it suddenly left him, passport and maps of Italy in hand, at his little house in Pimlico, just as he was setting off to a meeting with his dendrological friends in Florence.

How best to describe this indefatigable old soldier? He was shrewd, creative, and his memory was a marvel, he had an impish schoolboy way. Colonel Codrington of the Coldstream Guards became John the gentle watercolourist, the unstoppable traveller, the ingenious and sometimes inspired garden designer, the undercover agent, the singer, the leg-puller, the cheerful and bountiful friend.

Perhaps the most ineradicable picture of John is of his calm sketch-ing while a bus-load of dendrologists faffed about with their cameras and hand-lenses and Latin names on the top of some Andean or African pass. His watercolours went everywhere with him in a little crocodile case. At the end of the day, while his friends refreshed them-selves in the hotel bar and went over the day's finds, John, chatting and smiling in a corner, would be putting the finishing touches to his day's haul: five or six of his unique, simple but wonderfully expressive (and increasingly spidery) watercolours. I hope he didn't give them *all* away. It would be such a happy reminder to see a collection of them at a show next winter.

SWANSONG

Our swans have had to go. Having been the apples of our eyes for about 14 years, the loveliest things in the garden and to us the very emblem of Saling, relations became so tense that we have found them a new billet.

The trouble started when, having nested each spring for years on their private island in the duck pond, they decided to try the back drive instead. Mrs Swan had made a huge nest and laid her first egg within feet of the drive before we could – what? Reason with her? Still less could we reason with Mr Swan, who took to blockading the drive, attacking pedestrians and vehicles indiscriminately, and when not attacking stood with shoulders hunched in a passable imitation of a bull in a corrida, terrifying all and sundry. I couldn't go out without nervous backward glances to see if I was on the menu.

This spring we took the decision. The proprietors of much more spacious waters than ours, at the eighteenth-century Priory at Hatfield Peverel, said they would be happy to have our swans. One emotional afternoon we slipped both of them into sacks, each with a hole in the bottom out of which the neck emerged like a snake from a snakepit. It was surprisingly easy to do, despite our trepidation. The most danger-ous part, in fact, was the reactions of drivers following us and seeing two white snake-like heads weaving about in the back of our Volkswagen Passat.

The swans are in seventh heaven in their new domain. Ours seems empty without their arrogant beauty. Certainly the scuttle of the moorhens that have moved in to fill the void is a poor substitute.

—September—

ROGUING

A visitor remarked on the pure white foxgloves in the garden this June (some of them six-footers, with such a soaking to urge them on) and wondered where we had bought the seeds. The answer is that we didn't: we have simply taken a close look at each volunteer foxglove seedling and weeded out the mauve (which originally, of course, were vastly in the majority).

It was Graham Stuart Thomas who taught us the trick. Even when they are a mere inch across, the leaf stalks of each seedling are either pure white or faintly stained with purple. Simply pull up any that show a purple inclination and the white strain will take over; ghostly spires in the midsummer dusk.

STILL WATERS

The pleasures of the old fishpond (in Essex-speak, 'moat') in Trad's garden have up to now stopped at the surface – above the surface, that is. Ducks (and formerly swans) have swum, frogs plopped, trees reflected in a variously shiny mirror, but the presence of fish beneath, except for the occasional periscope of a nuclear carp, has been more a matter of faith than of the evidence of one's eyes.

Suddenly, and it seems miraculously, faith has been rewarded. I walked out one morning in June, a fresh morning after a heavy rain, to discourage the moorhens from drowning the ducklings, and felt like the chap in the Gospel from whose eyes the scales fell. Instead of an opaque surface I beheld the very depths of the waters, and in them things swimming innumerable.

What had been murk had suddenly turned to glass. Windsor soup had become consommé. The pond, I am trying to say, by whatever agency, natural or divine, was clear, and there, in numbers I had never imagined, were all my fish.

What had happened? The only explanation I can think of is that the cascade we built last year, which has been recycling the water for nine months now, has introduced enough oxygen to tip the balance between thick and clear. Perhaps the departure of the swans has also contributed. Could the heavy June rain have had something to do with it? I would dearly love to know.

The more so because the vision is fading fast. Half an inch of rain on a July morning seemed to initiate a new phase: a milky haze has replaced the crystal clarity. Now I can only see fish within a few inches of the surface – where the orfe, bless them, operate most of the time. I suspect the haze is being caused by carp browsing on the muddy bottom. Sometimes tell-tale clouds drift up in a fish's wake. But in that case why did they stop their browsing in June? Do I have a reader who is a pond clairvoyant?

Monsoon

June gave us no less than 5½ inches of rain. We can only be grateful that the monsoon was so generous to us; certainly its effect on growth has been almost embarrassing. My inclination towards jungle-gardening (plants that press against you and make you stoop as you thread the paths) is partly in reaction to our normal state of near-drought. When it pours for a month our paths can almost cease to exist: some had to be re-established with axe and saw.

But it was particularly along walls that steady rain reveals how little moisture the plants usually have at their disposal. I would usually reckon that three years of constant encouragement was needed to establish, for example, a new rose on the house. This year, by July, new roses were not only flowering, but making their first lunges up the brickwork. Where I have individually watered a new wall plant in a normal dry season, almost the only effect has been to flood the adjacent cellar.

— October —

Côté Jardin

With three months to go to 1992, are we all prepared to start Eurogardening? If it is true that 400,000 British citizens now own property in France, and presumably two or three times as many in Spain, Eurogardening is an established fact for a great many – and Members of the RHS too, I shouldn't wonder.

The evidence of their activities is already visible along certain roads in Périgord and the Lot, where old French roses almost certainly indicate a new English gardener at work.

Now Trad has joined the rush, seduced by the majestic calm of Europe's finest oak forest, the Forêt de Tronçais, into buying a parcel of the Bourbonnais almost in the shadow of this sublime wood.

The Bourbonnais is central to both the history of France and its geography. In fact, if you balanced France on a pin it would impinge (so say scientists who have performed such abstruse calculations) a few kilometres to the north of the Tronçais. As to history, the region seems to have stuck to its feudal ways until its châteaux outnumber its villages. And, of course, it produced the eventual royal family of France.

Château Trad, I hasten to add, is nothing of the kind, but a three-room farmhouse with various barns and appendages in the local rusty-coloured stone. It gazes south over the valley of the Aumance; not an impressive river, but a gurgly steam which has had time to cut a very respectable trench through the sand and granite, on whose crags perch various castles and chapels. Huge oaks, an old hornbeam coppice and shaggy brown sheep are the principal living creatures.

— November —

MORE THAN ELOQUENCE

Curiosity took Trad over to Newmarket the other day to see how lead statues are made. I had often wondered how such soft and heavy metal was handled to make intricate models in a foundry. The answer is with some difficulty – and above all at great speed.

Hugo Smith, a partner in the Bulbeck foundry, on an industrial estate on the edge of Cambridgeshire, showed me a dolphin – a component of a stately fountain – being cast; a process full of surprises.

A pot of molten lead, looking grey and scummy and not at all fiercely hot, stood on an electric heater, supported by chains and pulleys. At each end it had two long pole handles like a stretcher or a sedan chair. Beside it on the floor sat the mould, an odd-shaped aluminium box fitted with a funnel on top – also with handles.

Everything was ready. At the word go two muscular foundrymen lifted the cauldron by its four handles, took one step towards the mould and tipped the lead (now gleaming like dark silver) into the funnel. Also all over the floor. There is no time for niceties; the aim is to make it snappy.

As quick as they could move they had the cauldron back on the stove, picked up the just-filled mould, and emptied its contents straight back into the scummy pot. The lead hardens instantly, it seems, on touching the aluminium: the object is to leave as thin a layer of lead as possible to form the statue and to avoid creating a massively heavy and unworkable lump.

The mould was lifted on to a workbench, its various supports and component parts nudged away with a mallet, and there stood a gleaming dolphin, needing only a little fettling with file and chisel to buff away his seams – and of course the oxidation that gives lead its unique grey patina, in English garden light the equal of white marble in Italy.

I asked the statue-makers what they thought of the custom of painting lead, as practised in the eighteenth century and now revived by the National Trust. I had better not repeat their answer.

MADE IN HEAVEN

I try to note down perfect triads of colours when they occur in the garden. A triad is three colours which bear the same relationship to each other as primary red, blue and yellow, but unlike the primary colours share some pigments in common. Green, orange and violet are the mid-points between red, blue and yellow: instead of contrast they produce a sense of harmony. Sage, plum and buff is a less obvious triad that soothes the sight.

In August I was much taken with a chance grouping of a pale lilac *Phlox paniculata*, its silky flowers weighing down its tall willowy stems, with a stiff wine-red bistort *Polygonum* (I think) 'Superbum' – it was fairly humming with hoverflies – which reached up to the dangling citrus bells of *Clematis tangutica*. This is a triad in form and texture as well as colour. Also, I thought, in spirit; the feminine sway and lustre of the phlox, the male thrust of the polygonum and the priestly hovering of the clematis seemed to form a natural wedding.

— December —

THE CAPE IN WINTER

I wonder how many garden owners have lived in the same house and created its garden over a period of 50 years, and are still going strong, planting, creating and modifying.

I was taken round the comfortably English-looking garden of Rustenburg, a lovely Cape farmhouse near Stellenbosch, by Pamela Barlow, its still-active creator, on an early spring day in late August. As we stepped out of the front door under a line of tall shading oaks I said half-jokingly, 'You could almost have planted even these.' 'I did,' she answered, 'as acorns.'

Like many of the early Cape farms, Rustenburg stands at the foot of a great stony crag that feeds its springs and forms a dark dramatic back-cloth to the brilliance of its white gables.

The Barlows' garden, though, is in the school of Sissinghurst; of massed old-fashioned roses, winding walks of bulbs (agapanthus in masses) and peonies, subtly changing levels, pergola'ed paths (a Bodnant feel to this), cool basins of trickling water, walled gardens of grey-leaved plants and herbs.

August was not the ideal moment; it needed imagination to clothe the shrubs and fill the beds. Yet, chilly as it was, I loved the Cape in winter. The farms, their barns and fields and streams are far more visible through the black trunks and bare rigging of their oaks than in the density of summer green. The clouds fluidly grouping and regrouping round the mountains play beautiful games with pools of pale sunshine on green meadows and brown vineyards. As landscape it is surely matchless.

1992

—*January*—

LA FRANCE DES RONCES

Slotted in between the church and the village at Saling, with as much windbreak as we can muster between ourselves and the relentlessly flat farmland to the west, we have grown used to living without a view beyond our own boundaries. Which makes the panorama from the door of our new French cottage quite dizzying.

Sheep-dotted turf stretches away before us for 200 yards or so, then dips out of sight as the land slews off to the left down to the river. You catch sight of it again in rhythmic ridges of oak, dotted with wild cherry, to the right, but to the left all is dead ground until the valley floor appears, 300 feet below and a mile away.

You can pick up the course of the river by the line of poplars under the crag where the Goths destroyed a Gallo-Roman town in the sixth century. They lead the eye on to where the valley narrows to a cleft; the site the Bourbons chose to fortify with a near-replica of Corfe Castle. Three massive towers rising from the cleft dominate the middle ground of our view. It is hard to tell how far away is the ridge beyond, or the one beyond that – except that on a clear day you see the conical Puy-de-Dôme, 50 miles off, 4,800 feet high, overlooking Clermont-Ferrand where the hills of the Auvergne begin in earnest.

Did you ever wonder why Jack and Jill went *up* the hill? The more I study the behaviour of water on, in and under the ground, the more puzzling and unpredictable it becomes. It does seem odd that at this height the cottage has not only a well, but, as we discovered in demolishing the head-high brambles, a sizeable pond, too, stone-walled on one side. True, after three dry years, mud and bulrushes were the only evidence of water, but three hours scraping with the tractor and two downpours later we do indeed have a hilltop pond.

The evening sky filled it with fire the other evening as the mist rose in the distant valley. A sheep shouted. It is going to be very hard to add anything to this place. Just at the moment I feel even a rose bush would be gilding the lily. For how long, I wonder?

—*March*—

THAT'S SHELL...

What did we do wrong? We wanted bowls of 'Paper White' narcissus to fill the house with the sweet suggestion of spring at Christmas-time. We planted them in early October (the bulbs were already sprouting when they arrived in the post). By mid-November, in our cold dark cellar, the shoots were eight inches long and the flower buds completely formed. Long before Christmas the whole performance was well and truly over.

Where do they get all this adrenalin? The growers tell me that it is in their nature. They will always flower six weeks from planting. The only answer is to keep the bulbs, sprouts and all, in the bottom of the fridge until the second week of November.

—*May*—

NAIAD SURPRISED

I can't remember being so excited since I last had a Christmas stocking. Last week I found a spring – a beauty, gurgling darkly at the foot of a near-precipice overgrown with oak and hornbeam. I don't know how I missed it before in the days I have spent exploring the new Domaine Trad: a single soaring poplar wreathed in mistletoe beside it is a pretty explicit hint that there is water about.

It is almost four years since it rained as though it meant it in the Bourbonnais, so our spring is no slouch. In late winter the land was still looking parched, which certainly added to the thrill of finding running water. But there was something more elemental than that; something deeply stirring. If I had seen the naiad herself I could not have felt closer to the spirit of the land. In my excitement I didn't sleep a wink that night, as the dark water rose in my mind and poured its blessing on the ground.

—June—

A SIGHT TO MAKE ONE WEEP

When we watched the disgusting sight of the Serbian army and gun-
boats bombarding Dubrovnik last October it was hard to imagine a
more loutish and indecent act of vandalism. What we did not see was
something even more barbaric: the systematic destruction by the Serbs
of Dubrovnik's sixteenth-century arboretum, Trsteno, said to be the
oldest and one of the most important and beautiful in Europe.

Trsteno was laid out in 1502, 25 hectares of it, under Venetian
influence and before even Rome had its Renaissance gardens. Over
five centuries its collection became exceptional and its specimen trees
almost without parallel. Glorious great camphor trees, oriental planes
150 feet high, ficus, persimmons, tulip trees, ginkgos, casuarinas,
Mediterranean oaks, palms, cedars and citrus, olives and Aleppo pines
were not simple casual victims of stray shells; they were the subject of
deliberate attack with incendiary bombs and napalm.

Perhaps in a civil war where thousands of lives are lost mere gardens
(or for that matter historic cities) must be considered secondary in
importance. But this was not apparently the belief of the vandals who
attacked Trsteno.

As its curator has rightly said, this act of ecological and cultural
degeneracy needs to be broadcast and put on record. The Dark Ages
have not been left behind.

ON THE OTHER BOX

What is it about box, that most unassuming plant, that speaks so
deeply to the gardener; certainly to this gardener, but clearly to many
others? In America there is a thriving Boxwood Society, and many a
tear is shed (or my leg is very easily pulled) over the bush grown from
the sprig from great grandma's wedding bouquet.

Perhaps its great allure is the look of permanence that it shares with
well-clipped yew. A big old box bush is worth a lead statue for the air
of long establishment and distinction that it gives a garden. Beside box,
yew hedges are (or can be) frauds; a mere decade of good feeding and
they appear immemorial. Not so box, whose snail-like reputation is all

too justified. (Conversely, it is true, big money will buy a big box bush. Its root system might have been designed by a nurseryman for moving. Not so a yew hedge.)

Seventeenth-century gardeners turned against box. They found its smell fox-like and disagreeable, as some people do the sweet exhalation of the crown imperial, which announces itself even before its glistening green snout pierces the soil. According to Evelyn (*Sylva*, Book II) it was already being banished to waste places long before the landscape movement exploded. 'Exploded', by the way, is the term used by the grave Dr Hunter, Evelyn's eighteenth-century editor.

Why these meditations? Because I have been getting down to boxes with the specialist, Elizabeth Braimbridge, who grows more than 40 kinds at the Langley Boxwood Nursery in the middle of a wood near Liss, in Hampshire.

Do you fancy a weeping box, one with rosemary-like leaves, a silver-variegated one, a pair of perfect green buns or balls, a pale luscious-looking bush with new leaves the colour of a 'Golden Delicious' – even one that emulates a Lombardy poplar? For a deeply committed boxman (now smugly enjoying the bushes he planted 20 years ago) it was a revelation to see how much more there is to box than the green plasticine for model gardening.

And considering some of the smells they had to put up with in the seventeenth century, I can't imagine what they were objecting to.

—July—

DAMP DOWN UNDER

I had only ever seen Australia, before this March, in its apparently perennial costume of dusty greys, tan, tawny and hessian, bleached out under a colour-draining sun. But last summer (down under) after three years of drought it rained – and rained.

The Hunter Valley was a disconcerting sight; almost like Scotland, with pools reflecting the grey sky in every field, the gum trees a whole sheaf of different greens, bluish, russet and lettuce, where their parched crowns had broken into succulent new leaf.

My friend Len Evans, whose house, guarded by the stone heads he carves like an Easter Islander, commands the grandest view of the

Brokenback Range, had thought that his favourite tree, a massive old box-gum in a paddock below the garden, had died in the drought. In December not a leaf was left. By March it had a complete new glorious green wig for its head of bone-white branches.

In the Yarra Valley, just east of Melbourne, it was the same story in much brighter colours. Some of the best vineyards here are on steep slopes of red earth rolling down to Hoddle's Creek. The creek bottom is the home of the 'mountain ash', a eucalyptus that soars in silver slivers of bark to 250 feet, above glades of tree ferns. Intensely green vines, red earth, silver trunks and a dense woodland fringe of bright blue-leaved wattle were enough to make one rub one's eyes.

THE JOY OF WEEDING

It is only when weeds start to grow in good earnest in April that I remember again what a pleasure it can be to set about them – or rather some of them.

It would be a funny kind of pleasure that anyone could find in fighting the perennial weeds that colonise from underground. The couch-grass and ground elder school, apparently plugged into some main supply of incredible energy through their untraceable roots, is the most exhausting to pursue. Most infuriating is the oxalis persuasion; each plant a little landmine of bulbils that mocks you as you fork it up and it scatters its shrapnel all around.

Docks, of course, are wonderful at leaving just a tip of root in the ground, however carefully you delve and heave around them. Thistles are the same, though if you catch them while the soil is still moist a good grasp with leather gauntlets often succeeds in bringing them up whole. Nettles seem almost to give themselves up, roots and all, so long as you grip them low enough. Buttercups, too – with a little help from a fork.

But the weeds I look forward to are the superficial kind – the annuals. Deadnettles, fumitory, forget-me-not, shepherd's purse, fat hen, nipplewort and young sow thistles offer their soft foliage to the palm of your hand as if they know it is their fate. They smell green, earthy, minty, cressy. They make limp little mounds that stack up impressively on the compost heap. And the process of extricating them from among emerging phlox or agapanthus or asters, leaving trim shoots in clean ground, is somehow soul-cleansing, too.

WILLOW PATTERN

We are trying a drastic experiment on our weeping willow which is 30 feet high and, until March, almost as wide.

Taking, as it were, a leaf from the Japanese tree-surgeon's manual, we cut it back to a bare pole with half a dozen stumpy branches right at the top. The hope is that, producing sprays only from these strategic points, it will dangle long tresses of fresh green in spectacular vertical cascades, rather like the absurdly long catkins on willow pattern china – only more so.

The Japanese turn the weeping willow into a formal street tree like this. So far it is only sprouty scaffolding we have in the yard – with Trad up a ladder trying to decide how many sprouts is enough.

—*August*—

LA CHASSE AUX MOUTONS

Easter in the Bourbonnais gave me the chance to practise a new (to us) sport: sheep-hunting. Our predecessor at Château Trad had agreed to take his *troupeau* (there must have been 300 beasts) with him when he left. But somehow he managed to overlook a substantial chunk of his flock. We were left with some 30 bulky brown and black 'ovins' (the EC term) which not only started to multiply alarmingly but whose spiritual leader, judging by their voracious dietary habits, was Genghis 'Scorched Earth' Khan.

It is widely accepted that even a well-installed new fence is but a temporary obstacle to a motivated movement of sheep. Ours had one single motive: a change from their usual diet of grass, flowers, hedges and young coppice shoots. Restaurant critics to the last lamb among them, they quite reasonably identified anything newly planted as *nouvelle cuisine*. Just how they hunted down three measly little willows I had planted in 90 hectares of burgeoning France I would dearly love to know. For, next morning, their tender shoots had been chomped.

To my surprise it was not difficult to find a buyer for our ovins. The fun came when it was time to deliver the goods. The hunt began at midday, involving two sheepdogs, eight adults and a Land Rover. Bad light stopped play seven hours later, the huntsmen dead-beat (the dogs had retired exhausted at half time). Thirty-six sheep and lambs were in the barn, but four had defied all efforts, coaxings, chasing, and headings off. They had melted into the night.

As a quarry, sheep have qualities that demand in the hunter the combined talents of a sprinter, marathon-runner and a crossword-puzzle freak. An instinct for the unexpected is their strongest suit. Not only is their acceleration from a standing start in the dragster class; their ability to change direction, their road-holding and cornering are quite astonishing in anything so bulky. Team-work is their other winning ploy: a group of six, having followed the form book for a while and acted as one, will suddenly disintegrate into three pairs, sending the hunters in three different directions, then re-group in some impenetrable thicket and continue selecting the choicest shoots as though nothing had happened.

All in all a great day's sport – is what I imagine they baahed to each other in their richly herbaceous new quarters.

—September—

FAR CATHAY

Having been under the spell of Japanese gardens for so long, Trad arrived for the first time in China more full of curiosity than expectation.

Photographs of improbable piles of gouged and lumpy rocks had not been the greatest inducement, even with the help of Maggie Keswick's clear and enthusiastic commentary. (Her book *The Chinese Garden*, though now 15 years old, remains the best and most accessible text on the subject.)

To find a masterpiece, a garden on the grand scale and in apparently perfect condition, a place of infinite subtlety and suggestion, civilisation and polish, surviving in the very heart of Shanghai, was the last thing Trad expected.

To visit Soochow (disguised as Souzhou by modern spelling) was even more astonishing. Within an hour's train ride from Shanghai lies the Kyoto of China: a city of gardens with its origins in the eleventh century, not, as I had imagined, in a state of abandonment and disrepair, but with its shady avenues swept and even the water in its intricate network of canals purged of all rubbish by nets wielded from perambulating punts.

The first and indeed continuing impact of Chinese gardens is over-whelming – which is just what it is intended to be. It is easy to assimilate the tranquillity of a Japanese garden, whether or not you are up to decoding its spiritual symbolism. But the aim of the Chinese gar-dener seems to be to baffle and impress you at the same time.

The Yu Yuan, Shanghai's great garden, is a plot perhaps 10 acres (it may be much less, it is impossible to guess) divided into 50 or 60 spaces of varying sizes by a pattern of partitions, arcades, walls, doors, ponds, gateways, windows and above all rocks, designed to create an infinity of different perspectives. The largest space might contain a football pitch, were it not cleft by a ravine and subdivided by two substantial pavilions and a gazebo. The smallest is a claustrophobic grotto where only one can pass at a time.

At each turn a new picture as deliberate as a design on a plate pre-sents itself – or rather a choice of pictures, since there is such a plethora of elements to focus on.

The total effect could be likened to a curiously condensed, absurdly picturesque village with the quality of craftmanship of a palace. It stretches the definition of a garden as far as it will go – certainly far beyond horticulture. Yet what other word is there for such man-made delight?

– October –

MAKING THE GREEN ONE RED

Landscape painters have always been aware of what a single brushmark of scarlet will do to a scene that is predominantly green. The resulting red-coated horsemen and anglers, red-smocked harvesters or red-sashed dancers provide the voltage for paintings as different as Claudes, Cotmans and Corots.

I look from my study window down a funnel-shaped vista 200 yards long, always interesting (to me) for the gentle feathering of poplars and the antics of wildfowl, the stiffness of a cedar and the sombre richness of a yew hedge. A single silver willow (very Corot-like, this) animates the back-ground architecture of the poplar walk.

But how the voltage picks up in July when an eight foot line of scarlet *Antholyza paniculata* slashes into the middle ground along the bank of the pond. (Modernists know this plant as *Curtonus*; to the uncertain the best reference is to *Crocosmia*, or *Montbretia*: it is a bold and dashing version of the same design.)

The effect is of an open fan of light green with a broad scarlet fringe dipping down the bank. Oddly enough the eye does not so much focus on it as feel its radiance revving up the various tones of green, of shapes and shades, in the whole vista.

— November —

HIGHLY COMMENDED

I was sad not to be able to attend the fifth Beadnell Alternative Flower Show in Northumberland this year. These were some of the competition categories: least interesting cactus; super weed; drowning's too good for it (aquatic class); most misshapen vegetable; most unusually scented plant; least-tempting home-made sweet; most unusual home-made sweet; most imaginative use of a flower pot.

Children were challenged by the biggest slug or snail, while the lucky compost dip and ten-gnome bowling were for all the family.

The 'usual rules' applied: cheating will win extra points; this year's judge has even less qualifications; entries must be removed by 5pm. (The Health Inspector is due at 5.30 and the ladies downhill swimming team has the hall booked for 6.00.)

1993

—*January*—

THE OTHER CHIC

What started 10 years ago as a modest meeting of plant-lovers and nurserymen in the park of a château just south of Paris has blossomed today into the Chelsea of France. (*Libération* expresses it slightly differently: 'Le Festival de Cannes bi-annuel des plantes'.)

Trad, shamefaced at having missed the first nine years, was caught up in the happy throng of the autumn *journées des plantes*; three days in mid-October. The weather was perfect, the setting glorious, and any lingering ideas about the narrowness of French gardening ideas evaporated in the wonderful variety of plants on display.

Courson is a seventeenth-century château of brick and stone, cool and formal at first sight, but the home of two remarkable enthusiasts, Patrice and Hélène Fustier, whose love of plants has evidently won the admiration of *tout Paris*. Their creation is an entrancing blend of flower show, garden party and flea-market among the stately planes of a *parc à l'anglaise*, spilling out from the stables (rare books, herbs, dried and conservatory plants) into the cobbled yard and away into the shrubberies. Last autumn 140 stands displayed everything from rare oaks and maples to statues and conservatories, from alpines to botanical and architectural drawings.

Far from a banal repetition of the same popular plants, Courson was as tempting as a three-star *carte*. Specialists from all over France (and England, too) had boldly root-balled outstanding specimens of almost unfindable trees and shrubs (some of them wilting sadly, it must be said, in the bright sunlight) for Parisians to lug off home in their Range Rovers.

The 'jury' (under the presidency of Roy Lancaster) had meanwhile selected from among the exhibits *Les Mérites de Courson*: the golds and silvers in every category from bulb to tree, grouped to make a show-stopper at the entrance.

Courson is a must-visit for British gardeners with more than a passing interest in what goes on beyond the Channel.

I only have one suggestion to offer to the exhibitors. The relentless logic of the French post code is incomprehensible to anyone who has not memorized the numbers of France's ninety-odd *départements*. Thus a nursery identifies its whereabouts with a meaningless 32360

Jégun or 27220 St Laurent des Bois. Inevitably, before even considering its plants, you have to ask whether 32 or 27 signifies a balmy
Mediterranean *département*, somewhere in the Alps, in Brittany or
under the grey skies of the Pas de Calais. Would it be wasting too
much ink to name the *département*?

—*February*—

PLANT PURGATORY

There is a triangle at the north-east end of our old stable block which
comes as close as I can imagine to a plant purgatory. There are drains
just below the surface, no soil in sight but clay and builder's rubble,
permanent shade and bitter draughts. We installed a coal bunker there
and left it at that, sulking beside the back drive gathering the tougher
kind of weed.

Then I noticed how that unspectacular but perky plant *Sisyrinchium
striatum* seeds in the hoggin paths of the walled garden. Not only seeds
but makes jaunty clumps of its grey-green iris-like leaves in stiff confident fans. Its little yellowish flowers are not exactly picture postcards,
but its seed-heads, straw-yellow berries in spikes, are abundant and
look promisingly fecund. Would it grow in shade? I rounded up a
hundred seedlings, divided the fatter fans and took them round to the
dustbowl behind the stables. I planted them as best I could without
benefit of soil, sprinkled a bit of water about (more in the spirit of a
blessing than as irrigation with intent) and waited to see my plantation
wilt away.

By no means. Nasturtiums are quicker, but a year later the triangle
is a perfect porcupine of healthy grey-green tuffets. Their peculiar
habit is for stems to die back when they have set seed, but for the seed
to germinate and grow on on top, creating as it were a second storey,
not pretty but curious. I dare say the wonderfully uncomplaining
evergreen *Iris foetidissima* would put up as brave a show against all odds,
but I've already planted that all over the garden in shady places calling
for a spot of structure. To my mind its dark shining blades and red
berries look particularly well in winter with soft clumps of box.

ACER PATROL

Does anyone know why maples (not all of them, but certainly the Japanese sorts) seem to be so intent on self-mutilation?

I am talking about the completely unpredictable die-back of twigs small and large that constantly fills the crown of the tree with pale dead wood, inviting the onslaught of the mortal coral spot fungus.

Good growing conditions help up to a point, but even the healthiest trees need watching. Free circulation of air around them has appeared helpful (although they also like shelter). The only answer is constant watchfulness: a regular maple patrol to snap or snip off the dead extremities. I have come to know every bud of my maples – with immense pleasure.

—*March*—

WINTER BOTANY

These last rimey days, with mist frozen in lacy fringes on every twig, leaf, bud, tile, gate and cobweb, have been like a new pair of spectacles. What brilliance of focus there is on a frost-outlined object.

Details of plants that normally go unnoticed are now vividly etched in my memory. I'm not sure I could have told you if the leaves of a ceanothus that I pass daily had toothed edges or smooth ones – until the all-revealing rime framed each dark ellipse in acute silvery teeth.

The not-very-memorable difference between silver birch and white birch (the silver birch's twigs are rough to the touch) is translated into a much whiter, more frost-coated tree. Even grasses with slick leaves and grasses with hairy ones are distinguished by the sensitive touch of frost.

Winter is a good time for a non-botanist to make himself more aware of plant design; there is less to distract you, yet paradoxically more to see. And already, after a mere week of lengthening days, the extra quarter-of-an-hour or so of daylight has set the motor quietly running in buds and leaves all round the garden. Primrose leaves that were prone have arched their backs, even in frost. The daphne outside my study window has taken the safety-catch off its buds. On the shortest day I picked half-a-dozen sorts of catkins. Today it will be a dozen.

—*April*—

WHAT A COLLECTION

Anyone who had said, 15 years ago when the idea was first mooted, that by 1993 there would be more than 550 National Plant Collections up and running, would have been given an aspirin and a quiet place to lie down.

But that is the extent of the success of plantsmanship in harness: the recognition and encouragement of individual enthusiasms to give the country a reference set of plants in cultivation. Of course the set is very far from complete, but given the rate of progress it seems possible that most plant genera will have at least one 'home', appointed guardian (and hopefully chronicler, too) before long.

The National Plant Collection Directory for 1993 was published recently by the NCCPG at Wisley. Each year it grows in its scope and in the density of its information. At the same time the Council published the first monograph to arise from a National Collection – on 'Erodiums in Cultivation'. (Erodiums, for those with short memories, are close cousins of geraniums of particular interest to rock gardeners.)

The object of publishing such detailed and intimate knowledge of a small group of plants is to put on record everything that is known about its behaviour in cultivation, the character of its species and the history of its hybrids – even of those that appear to have died out. The effect of reading it – certainly on me – is less scientific. It is to make me want to plant, nurture and enjoy varieties I have never even seen.

AGONY COLUMN

My January resolution to have done with the 20 Irish junipers that have proved so spineless as sentinels in our walled garden lasted about as long as most New Year resolutions. I was touched when Eric Kirby, our strong right arm in the garden here for 20 years, overruled my decision. 'I'll fix the so-and-so's' was more or less what he said. 'Fixing' them was an extremely painful operation. It meant unwiring them to let all their besom-like branches flop, then disembowelling them completely, removing truckloads of dead brown (and extremely prickly) old wood and leaves. They were tower blocks for the birds: a score of old nests in each one – and scarcely less for mice.

Eric then cut off the top four feet and wired all the live outer branches into a tight cigar-shape less than half the bulk of the original. From now on they will get a strict clipping regime, and I believe they may have another 15 years of useful and decorative life.

THE NYMPH GARDEN

Ninfa never looked lovelier than this spring. When I wrote about it in October 1988 there were doubts about its future. But now Italy's – no, dash it – the world's most romantic garden is secure, and more perfectly gardened than ever. More, much more, about this anon.

—June—

THE KEY OF THE DOOR

Trad reaches years of discretion this month, a curious and not at all unpleasant feeling for a greying gardener. Years of discretion? A likely story. Comes of age, anyway.

June 1975 was the issue of *The Garden* that ran the first Tradescant's Diary. Eighteen years, 216 columns and nearly 200,000 words later some sort of milestone seems appropriate. I shall mark it by recalling to younger readers how that distant June saw the metamorphosis of the stately old Journal of the RHS (then in its 100th volume) into the bright-plumaged thing you have in your hand.

In the process it was felt (the old Journal habitually used the third person) that a more personal touch would appeal at least to the more frivolous element among the then Fellows. Trad was press-ganged to write a diary-cum-gossip column...and you know the rest.

'Why Tradescant?' was one of the first reader's questions of the new regime. The answer is simple. I was looking for a pen-name that was unmistakable, a sort of Atticus or Peterborough, but that spelt gardening – at least to the initiated. There was no Tradescant Trust in 1975; few know the name of the most illustrious of royal gardeners – and nobody still bears it, as I was at pains to find out. Very few even knew how to pronounce it (the accent is on the second syllable – a funny place to put it, I still think).